"In our modern ... it in the face of adversity, but ... gs of uncertainty and helple ... scribes how and why participa ... l, not only for doctors, but als ... nd medical students, struggling ... their patients' emotions, as they arise i ... relationships with patients."
–Peter Shoenberg, FRCPsych MRCP(UK), Honorary Consultant Psychiatrist in Psychotherapy Camden and Islington NHS Foundation Trust, London, formerly Head of the Department of Psychotherapy at University College Hospital London, UK

"Heide Otten gives us a very complete and rich view of today's evolution of the seminal work initiated 70 years ago by Michael Balint, with English general practitioners. This book reasserts the importance of the doctor-patient relationship. Be it in hospitals or ambulatory, the way doctors deal with their patients remains a cornerstone of today's medical practice. As a tool which aids doctors in this particular area, Balint Groups have continually increased in importance."
–Jorge Brandão, Vice President, International Balint Federation

"This book is a masterful exposition of the Balint group method in exploring the mysteries of clinician-patient relationships. Heide Otten, in calling upon her vast German and international experience, has written a superb book that provides a comprehensive overview of Balint group work, from its beginnings to methods, theoretical underpinnings and creative additions. Those experienced in Balint group work and those who are new to the method will welcome this new English edition. It is the book we have been waiting for."
–Dr Frank Meumann, former President of the Balint Society of Australia and New Zealand, Chair of the Accreditation Committee and former CEO and Director of Training of General Practice Training Tasmania, Australia

The Theory and Practice of Balint Group Work

Michael Balint's work grew out of a desire to analyze the doctor–patient relationship and improve diagnosis and treatment, and is now known and implemented internationally. In *The Theory and Practice of Balint Group Work* Heide Otten presents a practical guide to Balint groups and their relevance to clinicians in the modern world of internet diagnoses, distant patients and teams of specialists.

The book begins with a history of the therapeutic relationship and its influence on the development of Balint's work. Otten demonstrates how the sessions work, and goes on to look at the practical aspects of Balint group work with various professional and student groups, with participants of different cultural backgrounds and nationalities, and internationally. The requirements for leading a Balint group are then explored, and the book concludes with research findings and a look at how the practice can be extended to other professional groups. Case material from the author's own work is included throughout, and suggestions for additional creative elements such as sculpting, role-play and psychodrama are also featured.

The Theory and Practice of Balint Group Work is an essential guide for psychoanalysts, psychoanalytic psychotherapists, counsellors and medical practitioners and theorists coming to group work for the first time or utilizing Balint's ideas in their day to day practice. It will also appeal to others working in the helping professions seeking to strengthen the therapeutic relationship.

Heide Otten, PhD, is a psychotherapist in private practice in Germany. She was Secretary of the German Balint Society (DBG) from 1991 to 2013, President of the International Balint Federation (IBF) from 2001 to 2007 and has been a member of the International Foundation for Psychosomatic and Social Medicine since 2000.

Translated by Kaimichael Neumann and Heide Otten, with assistance from John Salinksy.

The Theory and Practice of Balint Group Work

Analyzing Professional Relationships

Heide Otten

Routledge
Taylor & Francis Group

LONDON AND NEW YORK

First published 2018
by Routledge
2 Park Square, Milton Park, Abingdon, Oxon OX14 4RN

and by Routledge
711 Third Avenue, New York, NY 10017

Routledge is an imprint of the Taylor & Francis Group, an informa business

© 2018 Heide Otten

First published in German as *Professionelle Beziehungen: Theorie und Praxis der Balintgruppenarbeit* by Springer 2012

British Library Cataloguing in Publication Data
A catalogue record for this book is available from the British Library

Library of Congress Cataloging in Publication Data
Names: Otten, Heide, author.
Title: The theory and practice of Balint group work : analyzing professional relationships / Heide Otten.
Other titles: Professionelle Beziehungen. English
Description: Abingdon, Oxon ; New York, NY : Routledge, 2018. | Translation of Professionelle Beziehungen: Theorie Praxis der Baluntgruppenarbeit. 2012.
Identifiers: LCCN 2017031438 (print) | LCCN 2017033825 (ebook) | ISBN 9781315147055 (Master e-book) | ISBN 9781138506992 (hbk.) | ISBN 9781138507012 (pbk.) | ISBN 9781315147055 (ebk)
Subjects: | MESH: Balint, Michael. | Physician-Patient Relations | Psychoanalytic Therapy | Clinical Competence | Group Processes
Classification: LCC RC506 (ebook) | LCC RC506 (print) | NLM WM 62 | DDC 616.89/17–dc23
LC record available at https://lccn.loc.gov/2017031438

ISBN: 978-1-138-50699-2 (hbk)
ISBN: 978-1-138-50701-2 (pbk)
ISBN: 978-1-315-14705-5 (ebk)

Typeset in Times New Roman
by Out of House Publishing

MIX
Paper from
responsible sources
FSC
www.fsc.org   FSC™ C013985

Printed in the United Kingdom
by Henry Ling Limited

Contents

PART IV
Results and opportunities   **105**

13 Balint group work with other professionals   120

14 Summary   125

    Bibliography   126
    Index   129

Foreword by E.R. Petzold

"What have the Romans actually done for us?" – "Nothing", was the laconic answer of one of Michael Balint's disciples – John Salinsky – expressed a few years ago at a lecture for the Royal College of General Practitioners in London, reflecting about the question however he revised his damning indictment. As a consequence of the growing power of the old Romans a civilization developed, which still shapes and influences Europe to this very day. Just think of the language you have or may have learnt at school: Latin, the mother tongue of Europe with its many "daughters". Or remember the traffic system and the roads the Romans built, in many ways superior to the magnificent motorways of our present time. Or think of the legal system, which remained unchanged until Napoleon adapted it to modern needs.

John Salinsky soon told us in London that he was not too concerned about the Romans. Instead he explained to us that he was really talking about the psychoanalysts, to whom general medical practitioners were highly indebted. He set out to disprove the widely held belief, that psychoanalysts had done nothing for medical doctors in general and primary care physicians in particular.

It was Michael Balint who set out to bring the two fields together, to find common ground and to encourage learning from each other. He spoke of "farewell" and "a new beginning". Good bye to outworn patterns of cognition and behavior and to the separation of the two professions. He recommended a fresh start to fair and mutual partnership. Balint was always open to and searched for novel solutions for problems and conflicts, which otherwise were often in danger of leading to feelings of resignation for the doctor and chronic illness for the patient due to lack of knowledge. Particularly in doctor–patient relationships, with the help of deeper trust, honesty, understanding and security, his new solutions would help to foster change, growth and healing.

As a successful and seasoned doctor and psychotherapist, Heide Otten is well aware that the relationship between a patient and the doctor is not only influenced by the subconscious feelings of the individuals involved, but also by the shape and structure of the health care system in Germany and elsewhere. She writes with experience and passion of decades of medical care giving and Balint group work with doctors and students. She has worked both in Germany and, at the international level, as far away as China:

> Key emotions in this context are fear, uncertainty, mistrust, helplessness, anger, work overload and insufficiency, which affect the doctor–patient relationship. The doctor, who feels over-burdened, will find it difficult to give a skeptical patient the attention and empathy necessary for a consultation climate of trust and openness. The insecure patient will not be able to reliably comply with agreed treatment objectives, which would be essential for successful treatment.
>
> (Chapter 2.8)

Balint knew of the power of preconscious and subconscious positions and he promised controversy in discussions. Balint (1957) wrote that just as we analysts speak very different languages ourselves, the patients speak to us in a diverse and different manner from us and each other. He stipulated that a kind of glossary would be necessary for proper understanding. In writing this book, Heide Otten delivers more than such a glossary. In analogy to the Romans, there is something else lurking behind. I can only try to describe this polyglot "something", through Balint's own language. His mother tongue was Hungarian, his scientific language psychoanalytic and ...

Balint wrote that he wanted to use the psychoanalytic language, the most effective one available to him, and then translate it into the other languages. I do not wish to use technical terms such as transference, counter-transference, resistance and therapeutic abstinence here. The language of psychoanalysis is an intimate one, in which two humans dive into an abyss of the soul, with the support of a rope woven from mutual trust. I attach this to the concept of primary love, the very first relationship, which a baby and a mother experience.

While Freud spoke of the mother as a "need-fulfilling object" in a rather distanced manner, D.W. Winnicott, a distinguished child and adolescent psychiatrist and analyst in London, and Balint's personal friend, spoke of the "holding function of the mother" and of being a "good enough Mother". On this healing summary of all those over-zealous, perfectionist efforts, which can sour parent–child or patient–doctor relationships, Balint (1965/2001) elaborated further that when objects appear out of an undifferentiated environment, the child basically has two possible modes of reaction and/or development.

He described those humorously in Greek, the language which taught the Romans what was not previously available to them: culture. In reference to the Greek and in grandiose anticipation of the neo-Freudian object-relations theory, Balint coined the terms "Oknophilia" and "Philobathia" (gr. oknos = the cave, philein = to love; batho or more exact baino = to put one foot in front of the other, to stride, to stroll, to walk). The most important aim of the oknophile person was proximity to the object (mother). For the philobat human, however, who is certain of the mother's proximity, the aim was to gain new and diverse skills and capabilities, in order to cope and survive in a rather complex setting and environment.

Why am I actually explaining this in a Foreword for this wonderfully clear and helpful book by Dr Heide Otten about Balint group work, as a mirror image of professional relationships? Is oknophilia a metaphor for the attachment to an illness or for a bond with this special type of group work? Do I love philobathia so much, because Heide Otten embodies it so clearly, always looking for new possibilities to integrate primary love into everyday medical practice – or to transform – for example with her conceptualizing the sculpturing technique for Balint work (Chapter 9)? Dr Otten has rendered outstanding service, more than anybody else, in spreading Balint work far beyond Germany – its adopted homeland – into the international sphere of influence.

Balint translates "primary love" – almost like a natural born Englishman – into the doctor–patient relationship, when he calls it "a mutual investment trust". What an understatement. He warned doctors of "the apostolic function", referring to the illusion – or "rudeness" – of pretending or believing to know everything better than the patient. To Balint, this was a patriarchal pattern of behavior. Today's model works much more from the premise of a partnership between doctor and patient. Patients are responsible for themselves, they have feelings, choices and responsibilities.

Doctors on the other hand are experts in knowledge and demonstrable data; they can show choices, concepts and solutions but the patients have to walk their individual paths to healing and wellbeing. Only I the subjective voice can say how I am and how I feel. Dr Otten speaks of "shared decision making". That is what I hear, when Balint invokes the concepts of "primary love" and "mutual investment company". We can all learn so much from our professional relationships. Balint promoted that process with what he called "training cum research in relationship". This training happens in Balint groups, the wonderful subject of this wonderful book.

This book could help us to overcome the unhelpful aspects of our time and of economically driven health-provider systems. In other words: to combine the genuine health knowledge of our patients, their own personal experience of disease and being ill, with the professional skills and knowledge of doctors and allied carers. This potential synthesis is somewhat similar to the combination of the strength of Roman civilization with the benefits of Greek culture.

E.R. Petzold
Kusterdingen, 9 February 2011

Foreword by John Salinsky

In 1957, Michael Balint, a psychiatrist and psychoanalyst, published *The Doctor, His Patient and the Illness*, a highly influential book which changed the way that family doctors thought about themselves and their work. In the preceding years, he had begun running seminars for London GPs in which they were invited to join a small group to discuss "the psychological aspect" of their work. The doctors were able to present spontaneous accounts of patients with whom they felt stuck, and with whom there seemed to be problems in the doctor–patient relationship. The resulting book was soon translated into many languages and Balint groups were started in other countries in Europe and beyond. Balint societies now exist in twenty-two countries from China in the East to the USA in the West. Their activities are coordinated by the International Balint Federation and there is an International Balint Congress every two years.

An individual Balint group consists of about eight to twelve members and one or two trained group leaders who often have a professional background in dynamic psychotherapy. A group, once formed, may go on meeting at regular intervals for several years. Short-term intensive group experiences are also available as "Balint weekends".

GPs are no longer the only beneficiaries: Balint groups have been found to be helpful to members of any profession in which human relationships play an essential part. These include hospital doctors, psychiatrists, nurses, physiotherapists, teachers, clergymen and social workers.

Although a relatively small number of doctors have had the opportunity (or the motivation) to join a Balint group, the medical profession is becoming increasingly aware of the value of reflective discussion in a small group of peers who are good listeners and who can offer helpful insights within a safe environment. The methods and style of these groups can vary a good deal, but the Balint group provided the model on which most of them are based.

Balint group work now seems to be rapidly gaining wider recognition throughout the world, and Heide Otten's book, now available in English, will provide interested readers with everything they need to know about the subject. Heide has been a tireless Balint enthusiast for over twenty years. As secretary of the German Balint Society she has played a major part in making the Balint group experience available to doctors and other professionals in Germany. She has also been very active in the international field, advising and helping to set up Balint groups and societies in many countries in Eastern Europe and more recently in China. She is, herself, a very skilled and thoughtful Balint group leader who knows just when to be quietly supportive and when to say something that will help the group to move on.

The book starts by surveying the history of the doctor–patient relationship from the classical era to the present day. Heide shows how Freud and psychoanalysis provided the foundations of psychodynamic theory which Michael Balint was able to use sparingly but very effectively in the development of his case-discussion groups. We then move on to an account of how a Balint group works. This section, like others which follow, is generously illustrated with vignettes of case presentations and group discussions. These have a liveliness and vigour which make you feel, as you read them, as if you are a member of the group yourself.

The next few chapters cover groups for professions other than doctors, for blended groups from a variety of professions and, very importantly, for students. Variations of the group which may include visual, dramatic and imaginative work are also described, showing that Balint work is capable of flowering and developing in different ways to suit the needs of the group members without losing its original character.

All this material leads to questions which Dr Otten proceeds with great authority to answer.

We want to know what it takes to lead a Balint group and how new leaders are trained and supervised. Finally we want to know if all this enthusiastic (and it must be said, very enjoyable) getting together with little groups of colleagues is actually helping us to do our job better. The research findings from all over the world are summarized, evaluated and discussed.

Whether you have personal experience as a member or a leader of Balint groups, or are just interested in finding out more about the Balint phenomenon, this book will provide you with an absorbing read and a treasury of information.

John Salinsky

Foreword by Donald E. Nease, Jr, MD

It gives me great pleasure to write a brief Foreword to this translation into English of Dr Heide Otten's book which appeared first in German under the title: *Professional Relationships*. I had the pleasure of reading the book when it first appeared and am very pleased that it is now available to a wider audience. Dr Otten brings a wealth of experience as a general practitioner with advanced training in psychosomatics, many years as a Balint group leader and terms as president of both the German Balint Society and the International Balint Federation.

Dr Otten aims to introduce the contemporary reader to the ideas of Michael Balint who brought into focus the importance of the interpersonal relationship between the physician and patient. In support of her aims, Dr Otten grounds us in the classical context of Ancient Greece, bringing us forward through various eras of scientific discovery to the present day. Through history, the centrality of a physician working for the benefit of the patient has remained. Dr Otten argues that evidence-based medicine and shared decision making, both of which have arisen since Balint developed his method, have not diminished the importance for healers to understand the pharmacology of their own selves, or "the doctor as drug" as expressed by Balint. This understanding is uniquely gained through participation in a Balint group.

Dr Otten gives a comprehensive description of how a Balint group is conducted with generalists, specialists, psychiatrists and mixed groups. These are each illustrated with examples of group sessions. Work with medical students is also described, including the Ascona-Balint prize for medical students, a cooperative effort of the Foundation Psychosomatic and Social Medicine and the International Balint Federation. Dr Otten describes the elements of leader training, including the principles set forth by the International Balint Federation and the German Balint Society.

Of course, given her grounding as a German Balint leader, Dr Otten has a distinctly German perspective, which is especially helpful as she describes the creative variations such as Sculpture that have developed within the Germanic Balint movement. Her international experience is also evident as she gives rich descriptions of Balint sessions held in various countries with the support of the International Balint Federation. This international context is also the background for contemporary research described by Dr Otten, on both the conduct and impact of Balint groups on their participants.

In summary, anyone doubting the ongoing relevance of Michael Balint's ideas and that of Balint groups should read this book. Dr Otten leaves no doubt that Balint work remains alive and vibrant, responsive to the needs of contemporary health care.

Donald E. Nease, Jr, MD
President, International Balint Federation
Associate Professor of Family Medicine
University of Colorado – Denver

Acknowledgments

Thanks to Werner Schwidder, who by his fascinating lectures at "Göttingen University" (1964–1967) triggered my lifelong interest in psychosomatic medicine and kindled in me the question, which followed me all my medical everyday thinking: "What do I give the patient, once I have taken the physical symptom away from him?"

Thanks to Hans Lauter, who encouraged me during my student practical at the Psychiatric University Clinic in Göttingen (1966) to move to Munich to do my doctoral thesis at "Max Planck Institute for Psychiatry".

Thanks to Norbert Matussek, who guided and supervised my doctoral research and thesis (1968–1972). He brought me closer to the biological scientific side of psychiatry as part of a pilot project on "Brain metabolism of inhibited depressive patients".

Thanks to his brother Paul Matussek, who through his lectures on "Psychotherapy of Psychosis" at "Max Planck Institute for Psychiatry" in Munich (1968–1970) encouraged me to think about the psychodynamic side of psychiatric illnesses. At the time this was a frowned upon sacrilege at the institute: "Are you also praying in the Matussek congregation?"

Thanks to Werner Stucke, who during my initial years as a general medical practitioner awoke my enthusiasm for Balint work – the analysis of the doctor–patient relationship. As a psychiatrist he was very grounded and careful not to psychologize every patient and every illness. He practiced and taught me a good eye for the balance of somatic and scientific evidence, social reality and psychological causes of disease.

Thanks to Margarethe Stubbe, who in her friendly manner managed to qualify missionary zest and at the same time saw the doctor–patient relationship as central in medicine without viewing it as a dogmatic panacea.

Thanks to Ernst Petzold, who with his profound knowledge and wide interest always brought up new impulses and amazing aspects in the discussion. He read my manuscript with incredible patience and gave me valuable encouragement.

Thanks to all my children and children in law, who are all young doctors in various specialties (Stephan in facial and maxillary surgery, Volker in orthopedic surgery and traumatology, Karoline and Annette in pediatrics, Tina in general practice, Julia in internal medicine and endocrinology). They balanced my overflowing passion and enthusiasm for working with the relationship with a pragmatic view of general everyday clinical exposure.

Special thanks to my daughter Karoline, who read my text with patience and compassionate and constructive criticism, and with her clinical competence added important thoughts and suggestions.

Also to the team from Springer publishing house: Monika Radecki, senior editor, planted the seed for this book in Lindau and watched over the growing project with Sigrid Janke, project manager. They were both kindly encouraging and very patient. Kirsten Pfeiffer proofread the manuscript with care and precision. Thank you all.

And thanks to Kaimichael Neumann, who mainly translated the German version of the book into English.

And another special thanks to John Salinsky, who edited the English translation as a native speaker and somebody who has a very loving sense for his own language and a beautiful style.

Last but not in the slightest least, I feel the need to thank all my colleagues at home and abroad, who have worked with me in Balint groups over the last twenty years. They shared their patient contacts with impressive openness and courage: discussed, fantasized, speculated and associated their perceptions with feeling and honesty. They have in the most literal sense of the word enabled me to write this book. In those fascinating twenty years I must have witnessed more than 3,000 group sessions with as many doctor–patient relationships at DBG (German Balint Society) meetings and International Congresses in Europe, the United States of America, China and Australia, and with students at universities; with groups in hospitals and practice settings; with homogeneous groups with participants of similar status and with mixed groups where members work in different disciplines. They were doctors of all ages and specialties, social workers, psychologists, music- and ergo-therapists, physiotherapists, teachers, clergymen and -women and nurses. Not surprisingly, because of the scope and philosophy of the group work, the sessions were always interesting and the dynamics never became routine. Each group, each presentation and every reported patient–doctor constellation presented a particular interest, hidden surprises and unexpected developments. Balint work is foremost creative and allows for spontaneity. As Balint recommended: "think fresh".

In all those years and sessions, I was privileged to work within a climate of empathy, tolerance and compassion among the group members. To all those participants I want to express my heartfelt gratitude.

Heide Otten
Wienhausen, 30 March 2011

Chapter 1

Introduction

There are two main consequences of our age of communication, computers, networking and fast-paced information technology. On the one hand the disparity between experts and lay people may have lessened. On the other hand however, the new trend has produced super specialists who know ever more about so very little.

We depend on networking and teamwork. Professional relationships consequently take on a new quality in a modern cultural context. Not that long ago, primary medical care was shaped through an intimate, trusting relationship between someone looking for care and help and a caregiver, let us say a family doctor. Today we rely on the interconnected relationships of helper teams. The patient in his system of friends, family and the internet is faced with a group of specialists taking care of his problem.

Those helping caregivers are possibly knowledgeable and competent but contribute to "the collusion of responsibility", as Balint calls it (Balint 1957). Who takes responsibility for the far-reaching vital decisions made by the collection of specialists? What are the relevant communication channels? Where is the place of the emotions and the importance of the role that they play?

The relationships between the professionals in the team also play a considerable role and affect the interface of patient and primary care doctor in everyday practice.

Modern medicine declares the creed of "shared decision making", which is often contrary to the wishes, needs and – mostly inaccessible – feelings of the patient, who wants to be looked after, held and relieved from responsibility.

This leads to an ambivalence on both sides and unconsciously influences the therapeutic alliance and the relationship. Significant conflicts may be the result.

These unconscious processes call for analysis of the psycho-dynamics underlying the relationship. Questions need to be asked: do I understand the underlying conflict of the person who is looking for help? Do I see what is behind the symptom, behind resistance and defense? What influence has my own attitude on this relationship?

And what have been the influences of the relevant social systems – family, work place, hospital, health care system, society as a whole – on the functioning of the doctor and patient as the core unit of health seeking?

In the 1950s Michael Balint (1896–1970) – medical doctor, biochemist and psychoanalyst – developed a method of group work, together with NHS general medical practitioners. The aim was and still is today to recognize problems in the relationship between a patient and a doctor and to find a better understanding of what illness really means.

He called the first group "a training cum research group" and therefore emphasized the duality of the underlying purpose. One aim was the further education and training of the helper, the doctor; the other aim was to research the effect of the helper on the help-seeker ("the doctor as a drug").

Balint approached his work with a scientific attitude: open in principle, capable of critique, permanently testing, correcting and changing the results. He demonstrated that knowledge and hypotheses about the patient and his illness are in constant need to be challenged, giving them a provisional and impermanent character. That has not changed in our groups today. We see the analytic group work as a method, that results in a combination of structure and spontaneity, with sense and sensibility making equal contributions, that always reveal something new and unexpected.

Today, the Balint method is also used in other social professions, to understand problematic relationships, to clarify context and to influence inner and outer reality. Teachers especially have gained benefit from understanding better and improving their relationship with students and their parents in a deeper way. The aim however is not to level out all disharmony, nor to equalize positions nor to remove intense feelings of anger, envy and impotence, but to bring them into conscious awareness and then use them to promote reflection, felt emotion and deeper awareness.

After all, what has been made conscious will be hard to push back underground again and can be openly worked with.

In this book I would like to introduce Balint's thoughts and make his concepts available. I believe it is necessary to start with a short excursion into the history of medicine to bring alive the historic changes of the doctor–patient relationship, to make the work and passion of Balint become clear and enable us to understand how we have reached the positions where we are today.

Initially, the influence which the healer, doctor or caregiver exercised on the patient was the greater, the less scientific knowledge was available. The importance of faith, magic, mystical hold, religion, spirituality and naturalistic perceptions was paramount to medical knowledge and its application in those earlier days of healing. The development and introduction of researched science and its application to medicine then redefined the meaning of the whole person in his context and totality quite dramatically. Nevertheless, we experience that interpersonal contact still plays a major role for human beings, who are, after all, social beings in a cultural environment, especially in the relation to the person, who is helping.

In Balint's words this translates as follows:

> The discussion quickly revealed – certainly not for the first time in the history of medicine – that by far the most frequently used drug in general practice was the doctor himself ... Still more disquieting is the lack of any literature on the possible hazards of this kind of medication, on the various allergic conditions met in individual patients which ought to be watched carefully, or on the undesirable side-effects of the drug.
>
> (Balint 1957, p. 1)

Patient-centered, trustworthy, empathic and well informed: that is how patients wish their doctor to be. Open, full of trust and understanding: that is how doctors wish their patients to be.

Working in an atmosphere with these respective attributes in the partnership, the patient can receive full benefits. Diagnostic and therapeutic interventions can be implemented, the doctor's skills, energy and knowledge can be maximized and harvested. The patient is allowed to receive attention and nurturing. The course of the illness is more likely to take a positive and productive development: "The doctor's personality and subjective interests may have a decisive influence on what he notices and records about his patient" (Balint 1957, p. 53).

Reality however does not always lend itself to dealing with each other in beneficial ways. We are lacking time and lacking patience and we are distracted by perceived necessities. Consulting rooms do not automatically facilitate understanding in the meetings of two human beings: too many inside and outside variables have their effect upon us. And often there is not even the chance to become aware of these shortcomings. What feelings actually influence and maybe determine the meeting? Can I utilize them, or are they in the way? Do I bring anger, anxiety, frustration and prejudice from other sources into the relationship? And what feelings are brought to me by my counterpart in the therapeutic alliance? What effect do all these emotions have if they are hidden and cannot be verbalized or at least felt?

There is much to be gained from exploring these questions.

And not only in terms of the doctor–patient relationship. Any professional relationship involving caregivers, clients, helpers and seekers of help, in any shape or form can become extremely difficult. Others too, for example teachers and students, solicitors and clients, pastors and congregation members, social workers, nurses, psychologists and their patients, all know how burdensome human interaction can be.

Burdensome relationships are stressful for everyone involved; to analyze and understand the difficulties can lighten the everyday load and help to prevent burn-out. Introspection is necessary: what are my parts, why do I find it difficult to connect with the person in front of me? If I can ask and maybe answer these questions, I will be privileged to learn a lot about myself. On the other hand, I will be encouraged to change perspective. What might influence or move the other person, what situation is she in? What might be expected of me?

We all know from experience that unsatisfactory interactions with our patients weigh heavily on us and take their toll in frustration, exhaustion, mental suffering and illness. To prevent these consequences serves what we call "Balint work" – named after its inventor.

Dankwart Mattke called Balint work "the most robust form ever of applied Psychoanalysis" (Mattke et al. 2009, pp. 83–86).

This book aims to convey my passionate belief, that it is worthwhile to travel this path and undertake this process of trying to clarify and modify our day to day encounter with others.

Group work is the trusted method of relationship analysis. Every group member brings their own attitudes to the presented relationship and helps to depict the perspective of the doctor and his interactions, as well as the patient's perceptions in his network of support, encouragement or distraction. All of a sudden or very slowly, a different picture of the situation is allowed to emerge.

This type of group work is practiced successfully in many countries and continents and it can be valuable to all professionals needing to reflect and explore and to find meaning in what is actually going on in their encounters with clients or patients.

Michael Balint published his book *The Doctor, His Patient and the Illness* more than fifty years ago. The literature on the subject is plentiful and I will give just some hints and references. My aim is to give practical examples and explanations to make the reader want to try this method, to read more about it, to join a group or experience it at a conference. More than anything else, I wish the reader to become a seeker of sorts, to ask their own questions and undergo their own personal experiences.

If I refer to the gender of a person, I will use a neutral form. If I refer to "he", I also mean "she" and thus follow the traditional convention.

Part I

History and basics

Chapter 2

The doctor–patient relationship in history

Illness and health have always been central themes for mankind. This is well reflected in our written history, in the arts and in literature.

The less scientific knowledge was available, the greater was the impact of faith, mysticism, religion, philosophy and naturalistic thinking.

The healer was believed to have magical powers and nature was said to be healing.

2.1 The classical era

"Medicus curat, natura sanat" – the doctor treats and nature heals, wrote Hippocrates (460–370 BC). He viewed the doctor as a supportive companion. It is not the doctor who wins over the illness, but the patient, the patient's own healing powers and those of nature. The doctor makes his knowledge and experience available. The course of illness takes time. To disregard this brings more damage than benefit. A good doctor takes that into account and encourages his patient to do the same. He accompanies and serves the patient with his healing art. Philosophy and Science are the basics of ancient medicine. Harmony is viewed as the most essential prerequisite for health. Illness develops from disharmony of the humors. The doctor helps to rebalance the humors towards the correct mix and thus harmony can be restored. The art of healing is to perform the right action at the right time.

The human being inhabits a lifelong position between illness and health; the doctor is the agent who helps the human being to hold the balance: total health is unachievable, total illness means to die. When the doctor can no longer help or heal and when death nears, he turns away and leaves the dying person in the care of the priest. The limits of the healing art are very clearly defined and respected.

Doctors in the ancient era valued psychological factors as a relevant factor in the course of illness and the healing process. Psychological factors are well considered in medical treatment. The temples served as sanatoria: patients stayed there overnight. Dreams and conversations played an essential role in therapy. Most probably the psychosomatic illnesses were treated in this way at the time.

We learn from classical literature that the basis of healing art lies in the loving and open approach and the honest desire to help.

The Hippocratic oath reveals:

> I will use all therapeutic interventions to the benefit of the patient and will do so to the best of my ability and judgment. I vow to never use them to the patient's detriment or in any wrongful manner. ... Pure and pious will I preserve my own life and healing ability ...

The Declaration of Geneva (latest edition 1994) states: "On entering the medical profession I vow unreservedly to use my life for the purpose of duty towards humanity ... The health of my patients will be the utmost priority of my actions..."

An important part of the rules and guidelines was aimed at the physician himself: there are prescriptions, which regulated the life of a healer: "The essential duty of the doctor is to heal his own mind and help himself, before he endeavors to help anyone else" (Epitaph, Athenian doctor during the classical period/Häfner 2007, p. xiii).

We know of a dress code and a code of conduct. The latter commanded the doctor not to harm his patient, to maintain confidentiality, not to perform sexual acts with patients and not to practice euthanasia. Surgical procedures were not performed by doctors: "I will to incise, not even patients suffering from Lithiasis, but I will leave this to the men, who perform that craft" (Hippocratic Oath).

2.2 Old Testament

The Old Testament, written between the 8th and the 3rd century BC, contains health regulations and behavioral guidelines which still play a role in orthodox Jewish life. The main emphasis rests on preventative care (cleanliness and God-pleasing conduct) rather than on healing and treatment, as shown by the quotes from the Bible:

And the LORD spake unto Moses, saying,

2

Speak unto the children of Israel, saying, If a woman have conceived seed, and born a man child: then she shall be unclean seven days; according to the days of the separation for her infirmity shall she be unclean.

3

And in the eighth day the flesh of his foreskin shall be circumcised.

4

And she shall then continue in the blood of her purifying three and thirty days; she shall touch no hallowed thing, nor come into the sanctuary, until the days of her purifying be fulfilled.

5

But if she bear a maid child, then she shall be unclean two weeks, as in her separation: and she shall continue in the blood of her purifying threescore and six days.

6 ...

(Leviticus, Chapter 12) King James Bible

And the LORD spake unto Moses and Aaron, saying,

2

When a man shall have in the skin of his flesh a rising, a scab, or bright spot, and it be in the skin of his flesh like the plague of leprosy; then he shall be brought unto Aaron the priest, or unto one of his sons the priests:

3

And the priest shall look on the plague in the skin of the flesh: and when the hair in the plague is turned white, and the plague in sight be deeper than the skin of his flesh, it is a plague of leprosy: and the priest shall look on him, and pronounce him unclean.

4

If the bright spot be white in the skin of his flesh, and in sight be not deeper than the skin, and the hair thereof be not turned white; then the priest shall shut up him that hath the plague seven days:

5 ...

(Leviticus, Chapter 13) King James Bible

And the LORD spake unto Moses and to Aaron, saying,

2

Speak unto the children of Israel, and say unto them, When any man hath a running issue out of his flesh, because of his issue he is unclean.

3

And this shall be his uncleanness in his issue: whether his flesh run with his issue, or his flesh be stopped from his issue, it is his uncleanness.

4

Every bed, whereon he lieth that hath the issue, is unclean: and every thing, whereon he sitteth, shall be unclean.

5

And whosoever toucheth his bed shall wash his clothes, and bathe himself in water, and be unclean until the even.

6

And he that sitteth on any thing whereon he sat that hath the issue shall wash his clothes, and bathe himself in water, and be unclean until the even.

7

And he that toucheth the flesh of him that hath the issue shall wash his clothes, and bathe himself in water, and be unclean until the even.

8

And if he that hath the issue spit upon him that is clean; then he shall wash his clothes, and bathe himself in water, and be unclean until the even.

9 ...

(Leviticus, Chapter 15) King James Bible

Illness was understood as test (Hiob) or punishment of God, which was to remind mankind of their relation to God and their position.

6

Now there was a day when the sons of God came to present themselves before the LORD, and Satan came also among them.

7

And the LORD said unto Satan, Whence comest thou? Then Satan answered the LORD, and said, From going to and fro in the earth, and from walking up and down in it.

8

And the LORD said unto Satan, Hast thou considered my servant Job, that there is none like him in the earth, a perfect and an upright man, one that feareth God, and escheweth evil?

9

Then Satan answered the LORD, and said, Doth Job fear God for nought?

10

Hast not thou made an hedge about him, and about his house, and about all that he hath on every side? thou hast blessed the work of his hands, and his substance is increased in the land.

11

But put forth thine hand now, and touch all that he hath, and he will curse thee to thy face.

12

And the LORD said unto Satan, Behold, all that he hath is in thy power; only upon himself put not forth thine hand. So Satan went forth from the presence of the LORD.

13 …

(Job, Chapter 1)

Leviticus, Chapter 26:

14

But if ye will not hearken unto me, and will not do all these commandments;

15

And if ye shall despise my statutes, or if your soul abhor my judgments, so that ye will not do all my commandments, but that ye break my covenant:

16

I also will do this unto you; I will even appoint over you terror, consumption, and the burning ague, that shall consume the eyes, and cause sorrow of heart: and ye shall sow your seed in vain, for your enemies shall eat it.

17

And I will set my face against you, and ye shall be slain before your enemies: they that hate you shall reign over you; and ye shall flee when none pursueth you.

18

And if ye will not yet for all this hearken unto me, then I will punish you seven times more for your sins.

19

And I will break the pride of your power; and I will make your heaven as iron, and your earth as brass:

20

And your strength shall be spent in vain: for your land shall not yield her increase, neither shall the trees of the land yield their fruits.

21

And if ye walk contrary unto me, and will not hearken unto me; I will bring seven times more plagues upon you according to your sins.

22

I will also send wild beasts among you, which shall rob you of your children, and destroy your cattle, and make you few in number; and your high ways shall be desolate.

23

And if ye will not be reformed by me by these things, but will walk contrary unto me;

24

Then will I also walk contrary unto you, and will punish you yet seven times for your sins.

25

And I will bring a sword upon you, that shall avenge the quarrel of my covenant: and when ye are gathered together within your cities, I will send the pestilence among you; and ye shall be delivered into the hand of the enemy.

26

And when I have broken the staff of your bread, ten women shall bake your bread in one oven, and they shall deliver you your bread again by weight: and ye shall eat, and not be satisfied.

27 ...

Illness is a warning and reminder to show gratitude and to recognize that mankind has to follow the Commandments of God and that they are dependent on his grace.

3

If ye walk in my statutes, and keep my commandments, and do them;

4

Then I will give you rain in due season, and the land shall yield her increase, and the trees of the field shall yield their fruit.

5

And your threshing shall reach unto the vintage, and the vintage shall reach unto the sowing time: and ye shall eat your bread to the full, and dwell in your land safely.

6

And I will give peace in the land, and ye shall lie down, and none shall make you afraid: and I will rid evil beasts out of the land, neither shall the sword go through your land.

7 ...

(www.biblegateway.com/passage/?search=Leviticus%2019)

2.3 Arab medicine

Based on the extensive medical knowledge of the Indians, Persians and Greeks, of the old Orient and on their own traditional healing from the desert regions, the ancient Arabs developed and transmitted well-founded medical knowledge. This was without comparison at the time; it was ground-breaking, modern, insightful and has been well documented. All this happened during the cultural and scientific peak time of Islamic high culture between the 8th and 13th century AD.

The Arab doctors used detailed techniques of taking a medical history; they had enormous knowledge of the use of natural healing plants and saw patients on structured ward rounds in general hospitals and specialized patient wards.

Central to all therapeutic interventions was the unity of mind and body. It is well documented that music therapy was given to help the patient's recovery.

Ibn Sina or Avicenna (980–1037) was the most prominent Arabian physician of the time. This medical philosopher was most renowned not only at home in Persia but in the West or Occident. His most popular book, *The Canon of Medicine*, was translated into Hebrew in 1279 and soon after into Latin. Even around the 1650s it was still considered as a standard textbook in some European medical faculties. The profound knowledge of Avicenna still lives on in today's popular oriental medicine. He was a physician and philosopher of contemporary "universal knowledge", had compiled all the available therapeutic usage of plants in *The Canon of Medicine* and had skillfully used these therapeutic tools to treat his patients.

The Canon of Medicine lists prescriptions of circa 800 therapeutic plants, extensive descriptions of diseases with reference to contemporary and classical medical teachers and a plentitude of Avicenna's own empirical observations.

Ibn Sina documented results from his own biological-scientific research and emphasized the close connection of emotions and physical condition. He also highlighted the positive physical and psychological effect of music on the patient.

One of the many emotional disturbances he describes in *The Canon of Medicine* is "lovesickness". He diagnosed and treated the Prince of Gorgan, who had succumbed to this affliction. He recognized a restless, quick pulse of the bed-bound patient as soon as the address and name of his female lover was mentioned. He prescribed a simple and effective cure: to unite the patient with his lover!

Monks in the Occident, the Toledo School of Translations in Spain and the medical school in Salerno (Sicily) introduced Arab medicine to the western world. It became an important basis of modern European medicine.

2.4 Middle Ages to the Renaissance

While the Byzantine and Arab physicians preserved the inheritance of the ancient era, western medicine was by all accounts relatively untouched by the wealth of skill and knowledge which had previously been accumulated. Very few Latin texts had survived and most Greek medical literature had not been preserved for posterity. Not until the 13th century did some influential and highly refined Arab knowledge of medicine find its way to middle and western Europa, via Spain and the Moors.

Through Italy and its economic ties with Byzantium/Constantinople the Greek texts were accessible again. The School of Salerno, one of the first medical schools in Europe, takes credit for the transmission of Greek and Arab medical knowledge to the western world.

The occidental teaching of medicine in the early Middle Ages mainly consisted of applied theology. Therapy happened under the guidance of monks and nuns. Nursing the diseased was the principal task and the underlying principle was charity (caritas). Diseases were seen as sent from God and healing as impossible without God's help. Healing powers were searched for in nature. Naturopathy was known as "cloister" medicine, the monasteries built herb gardens and harvested herbal medicines. One of the proponents of "cloister medicine" Hildegard von Bingen (1098–1179) is well known to this day. She described her concept of "unity and oneness" in her scripture on nature and healing. Wellness and healing of the diseased person, according to her, depended on handing over to faith, which alone could produce good works and a measured order of living.

The monks and nuns taught their knowledge and experience within the monasteries. Outside the cloister walls, "trading physicians" pulled teeth and performed surgical operations. Some women worked as midwives and herbal healers and were often castigated as witches.

The 12th century saw the foundation of the first medical universities in Bologna, Montpellier and then Paris.

During the Renaissance period the "cloister medicine" lost its primal position, but the established medical knowledge was incorporated into the new mainstream and was still highly regarded. The cloister pharmacies continued to produce herbal medicines as before. Their healers had previously taken advantage of books on herbal remedies from the classical era and Arab medicine. Now they furthered the herbal tradition with descriptions of remedies and started collecting the medical prescriptions in written form. The oldest example of a book in the German language about "cloister medicine" is the *Lorscher Arzneibuch* (*Lorscher pharmacopeia*).

It also contains the request that the healing arts be available not just for the rich but for the poor as well. The doctor is meant to be a health professional and companion and soother of all humans, irrespective of social standing.

The *Lorscher pharmacopeia* still carries some weight in today's context; the description of empirical evidence is widely seen as the forerunner of modern naturopathy.

2.5 Romantic era

Naturopathy built on the therapeutic paradigm of "cloister medicine" and developed it further. Christoph Wilhelm Hufeland (1762–1836) has been credited as its founder.

Hufeland incorporates "cloister medicine" into his "Theory of Vitality" in as much as he combines the self-preservation principle of the organism with the healing powers of nature. According to him and similar to the thinking of ancient medicine, therapeutic action lies in augmenting the individual's capacity for self-healing.

Other romantic concepts compete with each other and fascinate the thinkers and doers of the time, with medicine still founded in philosophy and optimism. Doctor and patient started to talk to each other and the doctor opens up to the patient, the patient feeling recognized. Taking a biographical history emerged as a technique; diagnosis and therapy are now based on a dialogue and the anamnesis. Equipment aids and practical tools for examination were still missing at the time.

Victor von Weizsäcker (1886–1957) commented as follows: "Romantic medicine deserves the great credit, that it prevented mathematical natural science from becoming elevated into a dogma and from reducing humanness into a solely biological theory of humanity" (Weizsäcker 1987, p. 14).

Weizsäcker brought back the romantic convictions of unity of body and soul. And he demanded the cooperation of doctor and patient on the same level: "One person in need, one person helps" (Weizsäcker 1987, p. 13).

The family physician or primary care doctor, who accompanies their patients lifelong, was born in the age of romanticism. He gives solace and hope, predicts the outcome from experience and supports the patient during the course of illness.

Magic and mysticism still carry a function, but increasingly the bio-psycho-social reality gained importance.

2.6 Industrial age

Knowledge gathered from biology, chemistry and anatomy increasingly found its way into medicine starting from medieval times. Dissection of human corpses revealed real evidence about the shape and structure of human organs and allowed conclusions about the functioning of bodily systems.

Industrialization in the late 19th century brought the invention of microscopy, the discovery of microorganisms and the invention of radiology, which in turn allowed bones to be visualized.

Improvement in surgical procedures and technological advances in terms of diagnostics and therapy brought a rapid development in medicine – metaphorically an explosive revolution.

Measurability now became the decisive criterion. "Feasibility" is the credo.

New bio-medical knowledge and therapeutic advances changed the perspective towards the functioning of organs and system. This culminated in the description of the human being in terms of "the machine model of the human being", which can be explored and modified with all the enthusiasm of the mechanistic pioneers of the time. The machine model reduced the person to a body as an automaton, which is steered by programs calculated and determined from the outside, through medication and surgical alteration. Illnesses were disturbances of functioning and had to be rectified. The physician turns into a technician, the patient into a body in need of repair. In this model the soul played no role or at best a very minor one.

2.7 Age of psychoanalysis: Freud, Ferenczi, Balint

The soul and its interconnectedness becomes the domain of psychoanalysis.

Michael Balint was born on 3 December 1896 in Budapest, Hungary.

At the time, Sigmund Freud (1856–1939) was 40 years old. Freud had studied medicine, written his doctoral dissertation on "the spinal medulla of lower fish", had worked at Vienna General Hospital; he had been a student of Jean-Martin Charcot (1825–1893) in Paris and had been influenced by his lectures about hysteria and about the effects of hypnosis and suggestion. In 1885 he became a lecturer in neuropathology at Vienna University and opened a private practice. In 1891 he and his family moved into Berggasse 19 in central Vienna, where he would live and work for forty-seven years. Together with his friend and colleague Josef Breuer he developed the "talking cure".

In 1896 – when Balint was born – he spoke of "psychoanalysis" for the first time.

When Balint started to study medicine in Budapest in 1913, Freud had already published important works:

- *The Interpretation of Dreams* (1900)
- *The Psychopathology of Everyday Life* (1901)
- *Jokes and Their Relation to the Unconscious* (1905)
- *Three Essays on the Theory of Sexuality* (1905)
- *Totem and Taboo* (1913)

Shortly afterwards he wrote *A General Introduction to Psycho-Analysis* (1917).

In 1917 Balint was given a copy of *Totem and Taboo* by a friend of his sister, his future wife Alice – a student of mathematics – and he was immediately fascinated. He had read Freud as a secondary school pupil, but now he was absorbed by this book and the *Three Essays on the Theory of Sexuality* which he discussed with Alice. She was in contact with the important Hungarian psychoanalysts through her mother Vilma Kovacs, and she had developed a special interest in "the unknown land: childhood". Alice was an active and open person, and had been corresponding with Freud's daughter Anna.

World War I (1914–1918) brought new findings and revelations for psychoanalysis.

Sandor Ferenczi (1873–1933) – the Hungarian doctor and psychoanalyst – wrote to Freud about his treatment of a patient with "traumatic neurosis", caused by the shock triggered by an exploding grenade. This way the tragic period of war promoted insights into the formation and theory of "War Neurosis". Ferenczi shared his thoughts on the pathogenesis of war trauma at a Congress in Budapest (1918), with the aim of starting a specialized polyclinic for patients traumatized by war. With the political change in Hungary under the Horty government however, his plans could not be realized. The further development of psychoanalysis in Hungary was terminated temporarily in the summer of 1919.

In the 1920s, further important works by Freud were published; he became internationally acclaimed. The language in which he wrote was appreciated as clear and understandable not only for medical practitioners.

In January 1933, the Nazis took control of Germany, and Freud's books were prominent among those they burned and destroyed. For the time being Freud underestimated the growing Nazi threat and decided to stay in Vienna. Ernest Jones, the then president of the International Psychoanalytic Association (IPA) got Freud to change his mind in March 1938 and to seek exile in Britain together with his family.

Finally in May 1938, Freud left Vienna and departed for London under very difficult circumstances. There he worked on his last books and continued to see patients in his new home in Hampstead/London until the terminal stages of his illness. He died on 23 September 1939 – suffering from increasingly severe pain caused by cancer of the jaw – with help from a morphine overdose administered by his doctor and friend Max Schur.

In 1920, Balint and his wife Alice moved to Berlin. Political change in Hungary had compromised his career prospects and psychoanalytical practice and research was deemed neither politically correct nor important. Berlin at the time offered the scent of change, freedom and intellectual independence. There, Balint joined the biochemical institute under Otto Heinrich Warburg (1883–1970) and achieved his doctorate in biochemical research. As part of his responsibilities, he tested the effects and side effects of medicines. Later he compared the doctor with a drug, whose effects and side effects needed to be further researched.

At the same time, he and Alice started their psychoanalytical training in Berlin with Hanns Sachs (1881–1947), a former colleague of Sigmund Freud.

Like many psychoanalysts at the time, Hanns Sachs was not a medical doctor, but a lawyer and political scientist. He had practiced law in Vienna, attended Freud's lectures and submitted himself for training analysis. In 1918 he moved to Zurich practicing psychoanalysis there and in 1920 he joined the polyclinic in Berlin.

In 1922 Freud attended the International Congress of Psychoanalysis in Berlin and presented his work on "the Ego and the Id". This was the first of many occasions when Balint experienced Freud and his teachings in person.

Balint left his beloved field of biochemistry and turned more and more to psychoanalysis. Starting from 1922 he treated patients at the Institute of Psychoanalysis and at the "Charité". Here he was allowed "to practice psychotherapy on patients with organic diseases. In this way he treated asthmatics and patients with gastric ulcers and published his findings. He sought his place as a pioneer of psychosomatic medicine" (Moreau-Ricaud 2000, p. 35).

Later, when working at the Tavistock Clinic in London, he made use of his experience in a group of general practitioners (GPs). In his book *The Doctor, His Patient and the Illness* (1957) he stated:

> doctors will be on the watch to prevent the patient from "organizing" his illness around an unimportant and accidental physical sign, thereby sapping in a futile and sterile manner both his own energies and those of his medical attendants. General practitioners will have learnt when it is essential to treat a "clinical illness" offered by a patient and when to disregard it and make a bee-line for the underlying "conflict".
>
> (Balint 1957, p. 287)

He tried to encourage the "psychological mindedness of the doctor" and thus to synthesize modern medicine and its scientific, technological advances with the knowledge of psychoanalysis. Psychosomatic medicine for him is "the medicine of the whole person". The patient consults the doctor and offers various symptoms.

Together patient and doctor find out what diagnostic avenue might be beneficial. The illness is an unequivocal part of the relationship, which determines one person as the doctor and the other one as the patient.

In 1924 Michael and Alice Balint returned to Budapest to continue their training analysis with Sandor Ferenczi (1873–1933). With his charismatic and particular style Ferenczi was immensely influential on Balint.

The Budapest school and Ferenczi in particular were renowned for freedom of analytical thought and experiment and for the explicit freedom to learn from analytical errors, analyze them and draw conclusions from them (Moreau-Ricaud 2000). This playful logic later formed the foundation for Balint group work.

In 1913 Ferenczi had founded the Hungarian Psychoanalytical Society, based on two core strands of competence, the therapeutic and the scientific one.

This concept of uniting therapeutic and research endeavors also formed a fundamental basis for Balint's work with groups of general practitioners, which he called "training cum research" projects and which he described in his book *The Doctor, His Patient and the Illness* (Balint 1957).

In Budapest Balint held seminars for medical doctors with the aim of introducing them to psychoanalytical theory so as to stimulate their interest in psychoanalysis and encouraging them to become psychoanalysts. In addition he wanted doctors to train their "third ear" to listen to patients and tune in to the difficulties they encountered within the consultation. The seminars focused on somatization and the reflection on the doctor–patient relationship: "The personality of the doctor often has more effect than the prescribed medicine" (Ferenczi et al. 1919, p. 11).

Another important thought resulting from Balint's work with GPs was expressed as follows: "If the doctor looks after the patient, who looks after the doctor?" This already refers to one of the most important functions of later Balint group work, the psychological health (mental health, psychological well-being) of the helper.

In his essay "Crises of the Medical Practice" (1930), Balint shared his observation that the doctor is easily seduced by modern technology and, consequently, is mostly interested in partial bodily functions. Examination of those functions was delegated to various specialists, and the overview of the whole patient and the human being was being lost in the process. He pleaded for the central role of the family doctor and wanted him to have training in psychoanalysis during postgraduate development. He wished that every patient could have a physician of his choice, to whom he could turn and would be able to trust.

The above essay was written after the Hungarian government had curtailed the health budget and limited accessibility of the health care system. Balint believed however that the policy had not been founded on the economic situation but was a consequence of a general crisis of applied science and medical practice.

These ideas of Balint's remain relevant in the 21st century.

The political situation in Hungary hindered the furtherance of psychoanalytical culture and education. Open exchange of opinions was basically impossible in a climate where Balint's seminars were attended and scrutinized by political policemen.

In 1939, Alice and Michael Balint and their teenage son (born 1925) emigrated to England, where Michael took up work in the Manchester pediatric hospital. In that same year Alice died from a ruptured aortic aneurysm. This must have been the hardest test of character and resilience for Michael. He lost his wife, friend, confidante and work partner, with whom he had shared thoughts, concepts, experiments and creative intellect. In the following years there are practically no more published works.

In July 1944 Balint married Edna Oakeshott, a psychoanalyst colleague working at the same hospital, but the marriage only lasted a few years.

Balint felt trapped in provincial Manchester and he missed the stimulus of the big city. For a few years he commuted between London and Manchester, until he chose to relocate permanently to London in 1947. There he took up a post first as a consultant and from 1949 on as a scientist at the Tavistock Clinic, a well-known center of excellence in psychoanalysis and psychotherapy. There he found his personal balance again and started the work for which he is now so well known in the world of medicine. He called that part of his life "my modern history".

Balint now went on a trajectory of his own. He had been trained medically and in the natural sciences, was familiar with the thoughts of Freud, and was convinced, as was Ferenczi, that the relationship patterns of early childhood were formative, and not only the sexual development. While working as a pediatrician he had studied in depth the relationship between a mother and a child in the offspring's early years. Resulting from this were his thoughts on "primary love" published in his books *Primary Love and Psycho-Analytic Technique* (1965) and *The Basic Fault* (1968).

In London, Balint met his later wife Enid, who had studied economics and social work, and was subsequently trained as a psychoanalyst. He worked very closely with her until his death in 1970. Together they developed the Balint group method, which Enid further propagated after Michael's death.

2.8 The 21st century

What has changed in terms of primary medical care since Balint's time?

Knowledge of natural science has rapidly grown and technical possibilities are increasing on an almost daily basis. Nearly everything is thought to be possible. Diagnostics and therapy have progressed enormously.

However – as Balint had already observed in the 1930s – a division has opened up between specialists and generalists, with the specialists being much more highly regarded. Consequently it has become more and more difficult to acknowledge and treat the whole person.

To counter this unfortunate development, in Germany we started to introduce the concept of "psychosomatic basic care and training" in the 1970s. This postgraduate educational program for doctors of all medical fields deals with the concept of psychosomatic illness. It aims to foster the practice of patient-centered consultation techniques and the restoration of a more holistic kind of doctor–patient relationship. Other countries have also striven to strengthen these ideas or are offering this additional qualification. The national Balint associations in different countries have been instrumental in supporting this development. Balint's suggestions from his essay "Crises of the Medical Practice" (1930) are thus being followed.

What does the doctor–patient relationship look like today?

It is influenced by political decisions for the health care system as well as by bio-technical development and possibilities. Any relationship needs to be seen in the context of the economic and sociodemographic background of our modern living conditions. We are facing a world of information overload for doctor and patient in modern communication systems, and an aging of the population in the industrialized world. The "crisis of medicine", which Balint described in Hungary in the 1930s, still exists today.

And the question needs to be asked again: is this an economic crisis? Do we have to ration treatment possibilities for financial reasons? Or is there enough money in health budgets or societies to treat patients to an optimal level? What is an optimal level? Do we provide adequate health care or are we displaying over-treatment in some fields of medicine?

How does the patient wish his doctor to be? How would the doctor like his patient to be?

"Shared decision making" is a popular phrase, frequently used in current thinking. The doctor informs about illness, diagnostic procedures and therapeutic options and the patient chooses according to his own needs and personal understanding. The patient is a partner at "eye level" and takes responsibility for decisions in illness and life. It sounds ideal but some have seen problems.

Doesn't the patient prefer – as we know it from the tradition paternalistic model – to place responsibility trustingly into the hands of the experienced physician so that he alone decides after a precise diagnosis which treatment plan seems best to him? The doctor shares only the most necessary information with the patient. This may arise from a position of patronage or from the intention to keep stress and too much burden away from the patient.

Juxtaposed to this there is the informative model. The doctor tries to present all relevant information in an objective and neutral way, including diagnostic procedures and therapeutic options with their advantages and disadvantages. The patient already has some knowledge about his illness from the internet, from other media and from friends and family. Feelings and individual patient experiences are not discussed. The underlying assumption is that the patient can sovereignly make the decision about himself and his life.

But is he really able to do so? Is the doctor really able to present all the information, without being influenced by his own opinions and preferences – what Balint calls the "apostolic function" of the doctor? And should he be detached from what constitutes his learnt and learning experience? Is there really an equal sharing of responsibility and decision making?

The model of shared decision making incorporates emotional and individual aspects into the process. Here, the doctor wants to be aware of non-rational aspects of the patient's position, and of his own for that matter, and encourage the patient to explore the emotional aspects of the situation. The doctor will be able to analyze his relationship with the patient and will be able to cope with the "fallout" from that privilege. He may also look at his own emotions, which no doubt influence his own interaction with the patient. The patient, of course, decides; it is his right and responsibility to have the final say on the decisions to be made.

Legal battles and court decisions are becoming more and more prevalent and more intense. The judicial climate shows that the doctor still carries a higher degree of responsibility than the patient. We expect him to be comprehensively informed, to share his medical knowledge with the patient; to be in tune rationally and emotionally with the patient and to be aware of the psychological influences of transference and counter-transference. We know that all actions, agreements and thoughts need to be well documented. The doctor who acts solely on his conscience may well find himself in deep water and incapable of defending himself successfully in the event of complaints and litigation.

The doctor–patient relationship is often influenced by fear of making the wrong decision and being reprimanded. "Playing safe", according to real and imagined guidelines and to taking litigious attitudes into account, might be understandable. At times, however, this leads to situations where important therapeutic decisions will be delegated to the specialists, who might not know the patient, might not be able to appreciate his wholeness, complexity and individuality. Balint called this process "the collusion of anonymity". This way, no judge or other arbiter can claim, even with hindsight, that something has been missed. Linked to the splitting and therefore refusal of accepting responsibility is the demand or the dogma of "do-ability": everything that can be done needs to be done for the optimal repair of the defective body.

But even when psychological factors are actually taken into account today, Balint's aim to treat the whole human being has often not really been achieved. The diagnosis of a psychosomatic illness is often only a diagnosis of exclusion. Then and only then, when no somatic cause can be detected, is the problem allowed to be of psychological origin. And even in that case, of course, the specialist for the mind and soul comes into action.

Approaches to integrated care have been made in the German health care system. Networking in different specialties is supported to improve the patients' supply and diminish the cost.

This however leads to conflicts with the principle of free trade in economic policy, which sees the doctor as the provider offering his service in return for the patient as a customer. Competing for patients and income and cooperating at the same time can be difficult. This definitely has an influence on the doctor–patient relationship.

Case management, in this context, refers to a fixed amount of income for treating a patient with a certain diagnosis in a certain time. This may however lead to a rise in profitable and multiple diagnoses and give rise to a situation in which patients with fewer diagnoses, which could put stress on the doctor's budget, may not be appreciated as customer-patients and might be discouraged from joining that particular practice.

Another concept debated at this point in time is payment by capitation fee or health premium. In this system, the care provider charges a quarterly or annual fee to registered patients regardless of the cost of any treatment. This system could also lead to profitable and less profitable patients.

The disease management program has however now been created to treat patients with chronic illness. Using the principles of evidence-based medicine, patients are treated according to structured protocols with the aim of coordinating the specialist's input and preventing secondary illnesses. Communication technology plays a major role here but so do considerations of health economics.

The term "evidence-based medicine" refers to scientifically researched and effective treatment methods, both in terms of individual decisions for patients and the ramifications of public health care. The need to use evidence-based medicine requires the doctor to keep his medical knowledge up to date with current research and to convey relevant medical data to the patient in an understandable and patient-centered manner.

This is where quality management finds its place; the doctor has to consent to a process of lifelong medical education and monitoring. The self-governing medical organizations have a duty to secure and control doctors' quality of service provision, but must also ensure the affordable provision of care to the public in general. The "Ärztliches Zentrum für Qualität in der Medizin" (Medical Center for Quality in Medicine) takes a supportive role here by supplying scientific research to ensure the highest standard of patient safety and patient information. It cooperates with the "Arbeitsgemeinschaft der Wissenschaftlichen Medizinischen Fachgesellschaften" (Working Group of Scientific Medical Faculties). The German Balint Society is part of this working party.

This particular structure of the medical care system not only leads to interpersonal conflicts and problems between colleagues, but it imposes on the relationship between doctor and patient. Key emotions in this context are fear, uncertainty, mistrust, helplessness, anger, work overload and insufficiency, which affect the doctor–patient relationship. The doctor, who feels over-burdened, will find it difficult to give a skeptical patient the attention and empathy necessary for a consultation climate of trust and openness. The insecure patient will not be able to reliably comply with agreed treatment objectives, which would be essential for successful treatment.

In an essay published in the journal *Science* in 1977 Georg L. Engel (1913–1999) criticizes the reductionist biomedical model, because it denies space for social, psychological and behavioral dimensions and perspectives of illness and medical care. He suggests a bio-psycho-social perspective for medicine and requests that the institutions of research and teaching ensure that this perspective forms the basis of medical care as a whole.

He expects that, as well as biological factors, the psychological development and the context of the social environment are both relevant when considering both the pathogenesis and treatment of any illness or disease.

One part of the latter aspect is the public health care system and rather prominently the special constitution of the doctor–patient relationship.

As we will now be looking at today's problems in the consultation room, both in the doctor's surgery and in hospitals from the Balint perspective, we will have in mind the historical facts and development, as well as the actual situation and current conditions, which influence the doctor–patient relationship in many ways.

Chapter 3

Development of Balint work

Let me take you back to the beginning. Michael Balint worked as Psychiatrist and Psychoanalyst at the Tavistock Clinic in London. His wife Enid had started group work with social workers to foster better understanding of their interactions with their clients. Michael had been asked to work with general practitioners as a consultant. Once again a war, World War II (1939–1945), had left traces and brought traumatized patients to their primary care doctors. Balint was well aware of the pioneering work of Ferenczi published after World War I. And Balint himself had treated patients with war neurosis and psychosomatic reactions to traumatization. Psychosomatic diseases occupied him as a researcher and he was interested to teach about psychoanalytic thinking.

3.1 How it began

Balint started to work with a group of general practitioners, which he called a "training cum research group". Exchange between colleagues was meant to teach better understanding of the patient, and also to explore the psychological background of his symptoms. In terms of research, Balint's aim was to investigate the "pharmacology of doctoring", "the effects and possible side effects of the doctor as a drug" (Balint 1957, p. 16).

Balint was convinced that "there was much more to the psychology of the consultation than was mentioned in the textbooks" (1957, p. 16). Furthermore he strongly felt that only general practitioners themselves could conduct the necessary research, because an observer in the consultation room would change the dynamics of the interaction too much for obtaining valid results.

In the groups, doctors report their difficulties with patients from memory, without using the medical record. With this approach, the listening group members get an impression of the affective resonance of the presenter towards his patient. And Balint emphasized the importance of not just the matters mentioned, but just as much the ones forgotten or omitted.

Following the art of psychoanalysis, he encouraged the group members to use free association when responding to the case study, to voice emotions, fantasies and any thought coming to mind without any censorship. He wanted group members to "think fresh", and to have "the courage of their own stupidity". To be able to feel free for spontaneous reactions and comments, the group atmosphere needs to be open and trusting. With feedback from the group the presenter thus receives a complex and colorful picture of his interaction with the patient and gains insight about his own part of the underlying dynamics. He can develop a fresh and new perspective of the problems and towards the patient.

The presenter will encounter his patient in a different way when they meet again, and – just like experience shows and Communication Sciences explain – the patient will also change his attitude – just as if he had been present during the group discussion, since he will feed on his different perceptions of the changed doctor. Often the next consultation finds a way out of the dead end situation, there is revitalized interest in the patient, the helplessness has ceased or diminished and there are new impulses for deeper understanding and treatment.

The basic question is: "Why is it that the relationship between doctor and patient is often so unsatisfactory and even unhappy, despite honest and considerable effort from both sides?" (Balint 1957, p. 378).

This question has to be looked at in a very individual manner, as there is no general answer and no master plan. The group will carefully enlighten and analyze each report and situation, which differs from case to case.

The questioning regarding unsatisfactory and unhappy relationships is a central one and needs to be raised in all helping professions. Why do I not get along with this pupil? What makes me angry when dealing with this client? How can I be more helpful and understand better what it actually is that my counterpart wants or may need?

That last question concerns affect and emotions and also some indication of self-reflection or self-critique. Traditional patient files might refer to affect and emotion of the patient, but not to the feelings of the doctor. Does the doctor just keep quiet about them or did he not perceive his emotions?

It becomes evident that the "entry ticket" into the doctor's chambers often is the patient's mood disorder or symptoms like pain, cough, diarrhea, etc. The doctor who knows his patients recognizes that there may be other difficulties hidden behind these presented symptoms. That again reminds us of what Balint said: "If the patient could visit the doctor with his conflict, he would not need the illness" (1957, p. 16).

In our group discussions we see that it is frequently the patient with a psychosomatic disorder who causes the most difficulties or problems for the doctor. Once a symptom has been treated another one appears.

These patients offer again and again new illnesses to the willing helper. Once both partners understand, however, which conflict lies behind the symptoms, and the patient is able and willing to search another way of getting along with life's difficulties and conflicts, he does not need psychosomatic symptoms any more.

Balint describes that there were members in his groups who were convinced that it is the right way to always examine the patient organically until a somatic cause was found, then treat the somatic symptom, and only by this approach would the neurotic symptoms stop on their own.

This error and mistake leads up to today to many unnecessary, expensive examinations and to useless operations and medical treatments.

The physician's reaction to the offered symptoms turns out to be most important. Even when the doctor already knows about "the true diagnosis" – the psychological problem behind the symptom – he needs time and patience to find the right moment and convincing arguments to share his hypothesis with the patient. And still the presented illness needs to be treated properly – e.g. the Angina Tonsillitis or the Gastritis – while at the same time the holistic angle is applied and discussed with the patient at the right moment. Listening to what people say, helps. The patient himself may offer the clues, when you ask the patient with the Gastritis, what made him "sour"? And the one with the Tonsillitis, what "diminished his defense"? The answer provided by the patient is then the key for further analysis. Is the patient able and willing to engage in an interpretation away from organics? And is the doctor skilled and trained enough to give answers to the patient's questions?

Psychotherapy after all is not just a matter of common sense; as Balint amongst others pointed out, solid background knowledge is necessary for successful treatment in a safe and secure way.

Is it worthwhile to acquire those skills and that knowledge? It has already been stated in Balint's time that about one-third of patients consulting in general practice do so with what was then called neurotic symptoms and cause problems for the GP. Today we estimate that half of all patients have mainly psycho-socio-somatic illnesses seeking advice and treatment in general practice.

Balint in his time raised the question of which option was more economical, either to treat the neurosis and hope the many minor problems would consequently disappear, or to treat those minor ailments with diligent care and ignore the neurotic foundations, since "we can not do anything about the neuroticism anyway". Balint's chosen answer is clear; he did however also point out the opposite nonsense of "sending every case of a fractured leg or measles to the psychiatrist".

Anyway we should not disregard the fact that the somatically ill patient will be psychologically burdened as well and needs a treatment focusing on both body and psyche to get better.

In today's context, lack of time and poor payment for talking with the patient are often brought as arguments to just do the bodily examination, and neglect the psychological conflicts behind the symptoms.

In any case, back then and today, "the conscious and subconscious life perspective of the doctor is an important factor when deciding which path patient and doctor will follow together" (Balint 1957, p. 298).

And this is another observation, which Balint made in his group and described in his book *The Doctor, His Patient and the Illness*. He calls this phenomenon "the apostolic function".

The doctor has his personal view, his prejudices, unconscious emotions, beliefs, which will lead to guiding the patient into doing what the doctor thinks right for the patient. As well he has a conviction how a sick person should behave, what he should hope or endure. He will try to convince the patient to follow his rules.

Balint viewed this missionary "position" as disturbing and not beneficial for the success of the treatment. According to him it would lead to a struggle between the two parties about commandment, perspective, belief and the "right way of life", consuming enormous amounts of energy.

It is important to Balint that his group work could help the doctor to reflect on his own background and dynamics and develop a critical distance and openness towards the patient's attitude towards life, his cultural background and religious beliefs.

Nothing much has changed since Balint's observation, that it is easier to convert the patient towards drug intervention than to engage him in a psychotherapeutic conversation, which is open with free floating mutual attention.

One of the most noteworthy effects of the group work – as Balint put it – is "a limited but significant change in the doctor's personality" after a while. And his experience showed, while lectures on problems and methods of psychological processes are valuable in adjunction, nothing can replace the actual process of group reflection.

3.2 The idea is spreading

In 1957 Balint published his book *The Doctor, His Patient and the Illness*. Its message found rapid interest in Europe and further away. Doctors from many European countries traveled to London to discuss with Michael and Enid and take part in their seminars. The Balints were invited to demonstrate their group work in different places like at psychotherapeutic conventions in Lindau, Germany, Sils, Switzerland, in France, Belgium and the United States of America.

More and more interested colleagues came to the meetings. Thus the "fish bowl" was created. For the first time in Sils, Switzerland Balint worked with an inner circle of sixteen participants – discussing a doctor–patient relationship – and others listening from the outer circle with no active group participation at any time.

This was adapted later on with the outer circle able to comment on the case and the group dynamics of the inner circle, which is experienced as enrichment of the group work.

The fish bowl is today used – in Germany and also in the international setting – for introduction and demonstration as well as for teaching purposes and also during Balint group leaders' training for observation and supervision.

The first national Balint societies were founded towards the end of Michael Balint's life, in France 1967, Great Britain 1969, Italy 1971, Belgium and Germany 1974. In 1975 the International Balint Federation (IBF) was formed with the aim to promote the importance of the doctor–patient relationship in medicine and to emphasize the need for any doctor to have psychological knowledge, whatever field and context he is working in.

Michael Balint died on 31 December 1970; his wife Enid stayed active in the field and became the first president of the IBF. She continued to lead Balint groups in England, added important publications and spoke on the subject in seminars and congresses.

3.3   International Balint Federation

Today the IBF consists of twenty-two national societies: Australia and New Zealand, Austria, Belgium, China, Croatia, Denmark, Finland, France, Germany, Hungary, Israel, Italy, Netherlands, Poland, Portugal, Romania, Russia, Serbia, Sweden, Switzerland, United Kingdom and the United States of America. "L'Association Internationale du Psychodrame Balint", the international, French-speaking organization is affiliated with the International Balint Federation.

There are also individual members from Brazil, Canada, Greece, Iceland, Norway and Venezuela.

The goals of the IBF are:

1. to promote and develop Balint training and research thereby fostering the interests of humanistic, psychological and psychotherapeutic aspects of clinical practice
2. to disseminate this knowledge thus improving the care of the public at large.

In furtherance of these objectives, the Federation through its Council shall have the following powers:

1. to arrange meetings, training and professional development courses and congresses
2. to publish and support publications on the Balint method
3. to participate in scientific congresses in these fields to promote and develop the Balint method and cooperation with other national and international societies and organizations.

Balint group work and its philosophy have spread in the last fifty years. Apparently it is still fascinating to explore the "caregiver-drug" and train its use. There are Balint societies worldwide, even in countries which are not yet represented in the IBF, such as Vietnam,

India, Iran, Turkey and Egypt. And although every culture brings its own charm and distinct peculiarities, the problems encountered in the day to day actions of the doctor–patient relationship are very similar in international comparison.

Kurt Fritzsche describes his Balint work experiences in Laos, Vietnam and China (Fritzsche et al. 2008). All three countries have recently undergone enormous social change, which led to mounting emotional pressures, to increased competitive strife even at school entry level and to individual stress leading to an increase in psychosomatic symptoms and illness.

The European Union sponsored the introduction of Psychosomatic Basic Care in those countries, facilitated by the department for Psychosomatic and Psychotherapeutic medicine of Freiburg University. One of the very interesting outcomes of the process was the striking difference in western and eastern culture in terms of the sharing of feelings. Asian colleagues in Balint groups demonstrated clearly that it is not their usual custom to talk openly about emotions. In particular negative emotional affect was not customarily allowed to be verbalized, related fantasies were forbidden and their expression of emotion would be threatened with sanction. The encouragement to "think fresh" was met with resistance and puzzlement. It was not easy to transfer our western Balint concept to the Asian culture. Introducing sculpture work into the analysis of the doctor–patient relationship made the emotionally expressive process easier and legitimate. In that sense we found a creative solution to a culture dependent scenario. We will explain the method more explicitly later on.

In the western paradigm the aim of our therapeutic work is to find a balance between emotional bonds and individual independence. In the East Asian culture we encountered the Confucian tradition: "you do not belong to yourself, you are part of many generations".

Delegates of the twenty-two national Balint societies meet twice yearly to share their experiences, participate in group work, to plan and discuss projects and prepare the International Congresses, in which interested participants from all over the world meet.

On the International Balint Congress – which is held every second year – new research findings and reports about activities are presented.

Current topics relate to the following questions:

- Is the use of Balint work measurable?
- What place does it have in postmodern medicine?

- What effect does it have in hospitals on the work climate amongst colleagues?
- How do behavior and attitudes change, when doctors during internship or further education take part in Balint work? How long does it take for those changes to become visible and measurable?
- Does it make sense to commit Balint work to all doctors? How do the obligatory groups work?
- Are there advantages and disadvantages of homogeneous and heterogeneous groups? Is there a right mix, if any?
- How do student Balint groups work? What are the specific problems in student–patient relationships?
- What do Balint group leaders have to learn? What influence do they have on the group process?
- What is the importance of humor in Balint work?
- What are the experiences of Balint work in other than the medical professions?

Rather surprisingly the research studies and the answers to the questions are similar internationally. There are no doubt variations from country to country, just as there are variations between doctors and individual patients. But the underlying principle of an analytical approach leads to a more or less strictly prescribed structure, which emerged over the years.

Chapter 12 will reveal more details of the latest research findings.

Part II

Practical aspects of Balint work

Chapter 4

How the sessions work

Today just as in Balint's time, ideally eight to twelve participants meet in regular group sessions. Those can be held weekly, monthly, every three months, in the evenings or on weekends with one or more sessions one after the other. For the discussion of one presented relationship 90 minutes are needed to really get to the emotions and to a deeper understanding.

The presenter introduces his encounter, his story with the patient. This could be a short interaction during out-of-hours emergency service, or an ongoing relationship from day to day care. He does not use notes but rather reports from memory. The way of presentation gives clues to the affective backdrop of the situation. First the group members listen without any questioning or interference, so the report is allowed to end as a unit in itself. Afterwards it mostly makes sense to allow factual questions for clarification and better or different understanding. Those could refer to medical and diagnostic details, particulars from the social history, to how the patient looks or to the setting in which the presenter works. It is of special interest which questions can be answered and which have to stay open, because the presenter never thought about it or did not ask the patient. It is the prerogative of the group leader which and how many questions to allow or whether to allow any questions at all. Sometimes the presentation immediately triggers intense emotional reactions by group members, and the emotional content of the doctor–patient relationship is immediately in the room.

Afterwards the presenter "pushes back" and listens to the discussion without interfering. He will get an impression of the feelings, thoughts and associations his presentation evoked. He might be astonished by some reactions, irritated by other aspects, he might want to protest, defend or clarify. By letting the picture that is painted in the group work on himself, he can look at his own emotional response.

He might feel misunderstood or misrepresented; perhaps he has withheld information and now feels neglectful or guilty; feelings of anger, desperation or incompetence might arise.

This can very often be attributed to the "parallel process" as termed by Balint, in which the presenter perceives emotions which might belong to the patient.

The group members take on different perspectives during the group discussion: the patient's, the presenter's, the institutions', the one of family members and so on. Thus a complex and fascinating picture of the situation emerges. The presenter might now recall certain key scenes or events, remarks or dispositions and can be allowed back into the group discussion; his additions and comments will give important clues to the nature of the discussed relationship. Again it is the prerogative of the group leader if and when the case presenter is allowed back into the conversation.

In any case he will be asked for his feedback at the end of the session. He needs the opportunity to describe his impression, perceptions and emotions during the session.

Balint work does not attempt to present a solution to the reported problem or to recommend a necessary course of action. The point of the group work is to uncover buried emotions and defended fantasies and to develop new perspectives and angles, with which to look at the patient afresh. It is important to incorporate new aspects, to make unconscious ones conscious, to widen the horizon and to leave dead ends of communication behind.

Only at the next meetings with the patient will the doctor be able to take in what has really changed through the group work. He will experience the patient differently because of the new insights and the patient will experience the doctor in a different light because the doctor's behavior and attitude towards him will have changed.

Two paramount aspects of Balint work are supervision and self-experience. The learning aspects of supervision are aimed at a "total diagnosis" and therapy, and self-experience in the sense of stimulating the participants to observe and reflect upon their own behavior and reactions towards the patient.

Transference and counter-transference take a central position in the dynamics of professional helping relationships and their perception is a task in Balint group work.

Transference constitutes all the subconscious reactions of the patient when interacting with the doctor. Counter-transference refers to the totality of subconscious reactions of the doctor, analyst, therapist or helper to the patient, and especially to the patient's trans-ference. Looking at one's own counter-transference can make the own unconscious – as Freud puts it – "the very instrument to analyze the manifestations of the unconscious of the other", here the patient.

In Balint work it may lead to the question: "What does the patient do to the doctor?" The doctor might for example be very motherly or sarcastic or overly caring to a degree unusual for him. An interpreta-tion could be that the patient unconsciously signals that he feels like a child, looking for a mother, that he does not like himself or is not able to look after himself. And these signals sent from the patient are incorporated into the unconscious of the doctor, who then acts accordingly. To realize these processes must now be the first step in making use of them for communication and for understanding prob-lems in the relationship.

The Balint group encourages participants to immerse themselves fully into the presented doctor–patient relationship and also to reg-ister and reflect upon their own reactions, emotions and thoughts arising from it during the group discussion. In this way, counter-transference becomes apparent and can be consciously incorporated into further interaction with the patient.

The technique of free association primarily includes the area of pre-conscious themes. The presenter already gives hints "between the lines" in his report.

In that sense Balint work is not simply the practice of prescribed new attitudes but rather the voluntary change of inner positions and attitudes. Balint spoke of the "limited though considerable change in the personality" (Balint 1957, p. 257) and Arthur Trenkel, a Swiss analyst, of "the switch of attitude" ("Umstellung der Einstellung", Trenkel 1998). The participant becomes aware of reactions and pre-viously unconscious behaviors, his perception grows and he will experience and share relationships in a different way.

In an ongoing group the presenter will share how he felt with the patient at the next consultation, what may have changed with the interaction and possibly influenced the symptoms or the manage-ment of the illness. Often it will be said: "It was as if the patient had listened in on the group process."

Chapter 5

Balint groups with doctors working in somatic medicine

Michael Balint started his group work with general medical practitioners in the firm belief that they were the professionals who used the drug "doctor" in their daily work in a special way: "The relationship between the patient and the specialist is really a different one, more technical and even the atmosphere of the consulting room or of the clinic is very different from the atmosphere in general practice." And he added, "We have to wait and see whether it will be possible and useful to hold seminars in order to introduce specialists to the psychological problems of their practice; if it would come about, it will for sure be very interesting" (Balint 1957, p. 198).

Balint was correct in his prognostic speculation. A mixed group with specialists from different fields of expertise has proved to be successful and valuable. The doctors learn from each other and are allowed to – following Balint's principle, to display the "courage of one's own stupidity" – raise questions, which they might not ask their regular colleagues on the phone at the work place. Furthermore they show and develop increased respect for colleagues from different fields.

Balint described the relationship between general practitioners and psychiatrists as difficult. In my mixed groups today, I experience that the meetings are characterized by mutual respect and produce good results.

Of course there are congruencies; psychiatric patients also see a general practitioner, physician, gynecologist or dermatologist. On the other hand a psychiatrist's patient may suffer from diabetes or eczema and may have recently recovered from myocardial infarction or a cancer operation. The inter-collegial exchange between doctors from different specialties in Balint groups is always valuable and desirable.

An ENT doctor once told me:

most of the time I work like a general practitioner. Many patients consult me directly without referral from primary care with their sore throats, earaches, hearing loss and so on. I know their families, listen to their concerns and problems and see rather a lot of psychosomatic symptoms.

This no doubt holds true for other specialists, too, like dermatologists, gynecologists, cardiologists, pediatricians, urologists, psychiatrists or dentists. They do not only engage in highly specialized, technical investigations or treatments, but work at a human level and in interpersonal relationships.

Our aim is to understand and possibly improve those very relationships with the patient, for his benefit and also for our own wellbeing and satisfaction. Some practical accounts will support this.

Example I

A young colleague recently started as junior partner in a rural practice as general practitioner. He tells the group about a 70-year-old patient from the neighboring village, whom he first saw when the senior doctor had been away. The patient is a mostly healthy looking farmer who does not talk much. The doctor likes him. The medical history is quickly taken and the young doctor listens carefully to the description of the acute symptoms. The patient complains of breathlessness and chest pain. An ECG reveals some rhythm disturbance, which concerns the doctor. He suggests admitting the patient to the hospital for further diagnostic procedures and initiation of therapy. Admission is categorically refused by the patient. The doctor speaks of further problems and complications, which could arise if further diagnostic clarity cannot be achieved, but the patient remains firm in his refusal for admission and makes it clear that he will not even take any oral medication. The doctor feels that the patient does not even listen to him any longer and does not trust him either. Following this first encounter, the patient consulted every now and then with minor complaints like a cough or simple back pain. The heart beat irregularities have subsided on their own. Ever since their first meeting the doctor feels or perceives a mistrustful patient and believes that he would have preferred to be seen by the senior partner. This makes the doctor feel somewhat insecure. And he shares with the group that so far he seems to have failed to gain any recognition or respect from the patient which no doubt would be necessary for a more continuous or long lasting doctor–patient relationship.

The Balint group members, all mostly young doctors shortly prior to or after starting practice partnership, showed empathy for the situation. Almost everyone else had felt similar difficulties as "a beginner", with patients, who did not think highly of the young doctor's skills and experience. An older colleague also recalled her encounter with her first patient many years ago: "That is something you never forget." After some discussion about how the difficult situation could possibly be improved by the doctor, attention shifted to the patient's situation. What had moved him to see a doctor? What had happened at home before the symptoms started? Had he been sent to the doctor by his wife or children? Was he afraid? How had he received the message of ECG abnormalities? How had he perceived the young doctor who had wanted to admit him to hospital immediately? And what were his feelings when he left the practice to go home?

For the presenting doctor, one question became prominent during the group discussion: what had prevented the patient from agreeing to a hospital admission? What was so important that he had refused? The doctor had not even thought about asking the patient in the situation and not until this moment. He decided to put up the question at the next consultation.

At the following group session he reported with some joy that he had now asked the patient. It had not been difficult for him. At first the patient was monosyllabic, as always. But finally he told him the story: the 70-year-old patient and his son worked the family farm together. The son had a lot of new ideas and suggestions which the father did not like. Just prior to the first consultation with chest pain and breathlessness, father and son had a massive argument regarding the purchase of a new machine. The old farmer thought it was unnecessary and far too expensive but the son insisted. Towards the end of the dispute the symptoms started. He thought straight away that he might have a heart attack and had sought help at the practice. On hearing that the problem was not an infarction, but only heart rhythm disturbance, he had been relieved and wanted to return to the farm as soon as possible to supervise his son, preventing him from making nonsensical decisions. He had not even listened to the young doctor's further advice and recommendations; he was already in his own thoughts again, chewing on the problems at home.

> The young doctor realized that he – being the same age as the farmer's son – did not have a great chance to explain and convince this life-experienced man with his well-meant suggestions. The old farmer was a rather well-weathered man and stubborn; the modern hospital investigations equated well with the new machines that the son had wanted to purchase. The doctor now understood the underlying conflict much better and still liked the patient. He respected the farmer's life experience and achievements and his approach to life in general. After talking to the patient and putting to him the important question, his relationship with the patient improved and relaxed. The doctor accepted stubbornness and the right to self-determination. And the patient seemed to have gained some trust and had opened up to the doctor.

This example shows a typical group process. John Salinsky (2001, pp. 183–194) describes the group work mentioning three phases: 1. support for the doctor, 2. empathy for the patient, his story and his emotions, 3. reflection about the emotional interaction between doctor and patient.

In this group the participants started the discussion showing empathy with the presenter and sharing their own experiences, which made apparent to him that he was not alone with his problem. That leads to relief and to the ability to listen to critical questions such as: do you know enough about the patient, were you interested, did you ask what was necessary to ask? Fantasies arose, which opened him up for a new approach to the patient. He had been focused on the medical physical diagnostics, had himself become anxious about missing something or making a mistake. He wanted, for his own safety and for the benefit of the patient, the optimal treatment in the hospital. He was caught in his clinical thinking – Balint might have said "in his apostolic function" – that he was not able to look behind, question and recognize the actual motives of the patient, which brought him into this situation. The group enabled him to broaden his perspective. And finally he found out himself about how their emotional relationship had been constructed. To experience and find out oneself provides a much more sustained learning experience than listening to lectures about transference and counter-transference, about projection and defense. None of these terms have been used. They were not necessary for the presenter to understand the doctor–patient relationship.

Example 2

A female patient aged 40 comes to the neuro-surgical practice. She suffers from symptoms from her cervical spine and has already been examined and treated conservatively by her orthopedic physician. Now she wishes to have two discs treated surgically. Three other discs have already been removed in the past. The surgeon is not keen to go ahead with the operation; he tries to engage the patient to look at the wider picture of her apparently somatic problems, but the patient blocks that attempt completely. She does not have any problems or conflicts, she states. She insists on having an operation. The surgeon explains to the group that his fears are that this patient will find some other doctor, who will agree to the patient's wish and perform an unnecessary operation. He asks the group if he could have dealt with the situation in a different way.

At first, the group members vent their own frustration that they themselves cannot prevent patients from having unnecessary and often harmful treatments, which renders them helpless and angry. They ask whether the patient does not have a family doctor and why she seeks specialist treatment on her own accord and without referral. Is that the self-determination, which the patient needs? What kind of a person might she be? How does she live and does she have a family? An orthopedic colleague remembers a patient with similar complaints who had a background of family problems, especially financial loads causing her illness. Her sleep had been restless and after tossing and turning she woke up with back pain so bad that she could hardly get up from bed in the morning. He explains that muscular tension and lack of relaxation would prevent the discs from recovering, and the discs as natural shock absorbers were dehydrated and ragged. Would this patient with neck problems have accepted an explanation like that? Would she have still insisted on the operation? Even if that specialist had taken more time and effort to talk to the patient, he might still have had to let go without being able to help her. This insight remained painful.

This is a specialist willing to see the patient as a whole. He does not confine himself just to his own field of expertise and the scope of technical possibilities. He is taking responsibility for the human being whom he encounters as his patient. The group respects his decision not to operate. His intuition was that the patient needed something

other than surgical disc removal. He did not know any details of the
patient's life story but the psychosomatic background was evident.
At the same time, his means of helping the patient to find another
way were limited. It is a quite common difficulty: patients often have
to travel a long path of suffering, symptoms and somatic treatment
before they can accept a psychosomatic, analytic approach.

Balint's idea remains topical and relevant: "If the patient could
take his conflict to the doctor he would not need his illness."

First of all, the doctor needs to consider that symptoms could be
caused by a conflict; only then can the patient benefit from thinking
about that concept and open up.

Example 3

A colleague from internal medicine reports that a radiological investigation for a gall bladder problem had revealed, by chance, an aortic
aneurysm in a 70-year-old patient. This had not been known previously and had caused no problems so far. The doctor was reluctant to
inform the patient of the finding as he wondered what effect the news
would have. Had the aneurysm not been detected, the patient might
have died from its rupture. On the other hand he might have lived a
long happy life, completely unaware of the problem. But now there was
this diagnosis; an operation had to be considered, in the knowledge
that, at the patient's age, the operation in itself might be life threaten-
ing. The doctor explained the situation cautiously, outlining the risks
to the patient and was surprised at how calmly he took the news. The
patient asked for time to think about it and to discuss the options with
his family, before making a decision. He then decided to go ahead. The
operation was taking place at the time of the Balint group.

The group showed a lot of sympathy for the situation of the doctor. Similar experiences were recalled by his colleagues. Feelings of
fear, restlessness, hope and doubt were mentioned. Then the thought
was voiced of how nice it would have been if the patient could have
talked about the situation with his GP, who might have known him
and his family well for a long time. The internist had seen him for the
first time and found it difficult to anticipate the patient's reaction.
Apparently the patient had nevertheless taken the news calmly and
the decision to involve his family seemed rational and well considered.

Maybe his fear of death was less than the doctor had anticipated? Was he at the age of 70 prepared; had he already dealt with death? Was it more a case of the young physician identifying with the patient and theoretically having to make a decision for himself?

He had a family with two young children and was in another stage of life. Thoughts like "carpe diem" and "postponing means loss of life" came up. The group felt like tuning in to personal values and spoke for a while about work–life balance, duty and freedom, pleasure and burden and their own anxieties, and considerations of right and wrong.

The group expressed the hope that the patient himself had found that balance in life and was able to accept whatever the outcome might be. And there was the wish for the patient to have a life after the operation, which was shared with heartfelt empathy.

After the session, during a break, the physician rang the hospital to enquire about the outcome of the surgery. The operation had gone well and without any complications. All the group members were very happy about this news.

Example 4

A female family doctor presented a 91-year-old man. She had known him for thirty years and was familiar with the family history. The patient had lost his wife two years ago and one of his two sons six months ago. As a young man, the patient had experienced the war and had thus been traumatized by the horror he had been involved in. After the war he started a family at the age of 30 and worked hard as a diligent and modest person. In the recent past he had not seen the doctor often; apparently he felt well. He lived alone and was traveling a lot. Now he had a cold and just asked for some medication. The doctor noticed that he had lost weight and had bruises on his arms and torso. When questioned, the patient explained that he had stumbled and knocked himself, as one does at his age; that was not a problem for him. And eating was not important for him any more, he felt fine, he said. The doctor was not convinced. She offered to take him home, she had visits to do anyway and would drive to his neighborhood. She had been in his home before, and when he invited her in, she was surprised by the general untidiness of the apartment. When his wife had still been alive, everything had been immaculate. The patient smiled and said: "Yes I live like a student now and am very happy with that.

> I was not able to do so in the past when I was young. But it is never too
> late and I can enjoy it now." A few days later the patient's nephew –
> a physician from another town – called her to say that he was very
> worried about his uncle. His uncle, who was on a good pension, was
> now always in debt at the end of the month. That was unusual and
> the nephew felt that his uncle needed some structured support. Would
> the doctor please see to it? When she mentioned the nephew's wor-
> ries about money to the old man, he smiled and agreed that he finally
> enjoyed life and was spending his money. He did not get on well with
> his one remaining son, who did not understand him and did not look
> after him at all. He had decided to not leave any money to him. The
> patient seemed happy and content but the doctor still had that weary
> feeling, and that was why she brought him to the Balint group.

Already when the case was presented, the group members showed
mostly cheerfulness. They wanted to say to the patient, "Well done!"
They thought – that is how old age should be. The patient did not
harm anyone and should just enjoy every remaining day. The male
group members were especially in agreement with the patient's
position. The woman seemed rather more cautious and worried.
Eventually some group members raised more concerns, in particular
the doctors working in psychiatry: was the patient really able to care
for himself? Might he not be euphoric, silly, detached from reality or
even hypomanic?

Should the doctor take responsibility on her own or should she
involve a psychiatrist? On the other hand, what would happen if she
did? The patient would probably be forced into sheltered accommo-
dation and lose his new found freedom. He might not be allowed
to walk into town all by himself and his quality of life, which he
seemed to have regained, would be threatened. He might become sad
or depressed: what would have been gained?

The doctor realized during the group session that she had been
more afraid of being the object of the scorn and condemnation of
the nephew and colleague should the uncle come to harm, than of
the possibility of the patient actually coming to some harm. She
decided to monitor the situation and see the patient at regular intervals. She would talk to him and only intervene further if the situation
really became untenable. Fear had been replaced by true care and
watchfulness.

Example 5

A female gynecologist reports about a situation from an out-of-hours emergency clinic. A 13-year-old girl was brought by her mother, presenting with lower abdominal pain. While taking a history, the doctor noticed with some discomfort that it was solely the mother and not the young girl answering her questions. The girl was said to have had her regular menstruation for a year; she did not have a boyfriend and had never had sexual intercourse. The mother denied any other illnesses and taking of any medication. Neither the gynecologist nor a surgeon could detect any abnormal findings. Incidentally, the mother also mentioned that she had given her daughter the oral contraceptive pill for the last year. The gynecologist was surprised as there was no boyfriend and no sexual intercourse. The mother explained rather angrily that her other daughter who was 16 now had given birth to a child at the age of 14, which she now had to bring up. She would not want to endure that again and preferred to take precautions. The pill was prescribed for herself, and as she did not need it at the moment, she gave it to her daughter. The gynecologist argued that it was irresponsible to give the pill to a 12-year-old, who had not started her period at the time and for whom it had not been prescribed and without any consultation or examination. The mother did not take these concerns on board and as an emergency doctor, the gynecologist was unable to do anything about it.

The doctor was noticeably feeling angry and helpless. The group members shared her outrage about the mother and felt for the situation of the young girl. Did she now have to bear the consequences of her older sister's predicament? Wasn't there anybody who might take care of the situation? What if any chance had the doctor, whose job had been primarily to diagnose the lower abdominal pain of the girl? Would she have to leave it at that? Who would help the girl? And who was on the mother's side to help her as a single mother with two teenage and pubescent daughters and a grandchild, in a big city? The group members thought about their own families, their own well-protected children. They wondered whether their kids would be able to ask the parents for help in a similar insoluble situation. On the one hand the presenter was the professional who felt the necessity to avoid further hormonal medication of the young girl. On the other hand, she felt the burden of the mother in a difficult life situation and she empathized with the 13-year-old girl who showed her distress and suffering through a symptom, but nobody was talking to her. Feelings of helplessness, limitation and discomfort remained in the group.

A pediatrician, member of another Balint group, had in a similar case involved the authorities. Social services and a midwife regularly visited the family. But they had been unable to prevent the death of the small child from being shaken in helpless anger a short while later. It is important for a report and an outcome like this, to be considered in a Balint group. Feelings of bereavement, anger, guilt and failure are unavoidable and should be discussed in order to enable the doctor to carry on with his work, despite the sad outcome. And we are able to see a potentiating effect of such a report.

The other group participants know families with different but similar constellations and can choose to be more aware and reflective. They may be able to question their own actions or attitudes and accept that the possibilities to interfere are limited.

Example 6

A dentist talks about a patient, who started to see him on a regular basis, after a molar tooth had been removed and a bridge implanted. She complains of continuous pain for which he cannot elicit a reason. She had already been examined by other dentists and there were already problems with the health insurance regarding further remuneration: "I am already at the end of my tether when I see her in the waiting room. I have no idea what I am supposed to do with her." A consultation with a psychotherapist had been suggested, but the patient adamantly refuses to entertain that possibility, as she claims that she is not just imagining her pain after all. So she comes again and again to consult the dentist. "Attached to each tooth is after all a human being" (Stoffel 2003).

In the group, plenty of sayings come to mind, from "the people's mouth" so to speak "to grit your teeth", "the toothless tiger", "the poisoned tooth", "grinding your teeth", "tooth for tooth", "to fill a gap" or "not being able to fill or fulfill". Associating with these sayings, the dentist remembers that his assistant, who lives in the same village as the patient, had told him that the woman's son had been killed in a motorcycle accident. There could be a connection to the beginning of her toothache.

With this recollection the mood in the group changed. The atmosphere so far had been filled with tension, irritation and anger towards the patient and with frustration and helplessness. Now the group notices how little they had come to know of the patient. The gap is filled. They now learn that she had an adult son, would therefore be around 50 years old and lived in a small village. The patient gets a "face" and a story, the toothache fades somewhat into the background. What is the woman expressing with her visits to the dentist? Why does she continue to consult him, when he clearly has not been able to help her any more? She is complaining and receives some acknowledgment. How might it be at her home? Her family would have suffered bereavement and probably will not listen to her complaints any more. No one can replace the loss or fill the gap in her life. The loss is painful. Sometimes bodily pain is easier to bear than psychic pain.

Balint asked in this context, whether it might be better sometimes to leave the patient with somatic pain rather than to intervene and rekindle the psychic pain. In fact we do not know whether this is true for this patient, whether the projection of the pain of loss onto a lost tooth held any merit. But the mood of the dentist had now noticeably changed during the group work. Sadness and pain will also diminish one day in this patient. The dentist is now able and willing to simply comfort the patient, whom he has known for such a long time and whom he likes. He will accept her pain, adjust the bridge, salve the gap every now and then and exchange some friendly words with her. He will "allow" her to return on her terms. There is now a feeling of almost fatherly counter-transference, which entails more patience and empathy.

Chapter 6

Balint groups with psychiatrists, psychotherapists and psychosomatic physicians

To begin with, Balint saw psychiatrists and psychoanalysts only as leaders of his groups.

In Germany today, however, Balint group work is an essential part of specialist training in psychiatry, psychoanalysis and psychosomatic medicine. It is now widely accepted that working on the doctor–patient relationship is a cornerstone of dealing with emotionally or psychologically afflicted patients.

A female doctor and psychotherapist talked about her experience as a member of a Balint group. When asked what she had learned, she answered that her perception had become more holistic: "I have been re-confronted with medicine and I am now more aware that psychoanalysis, maybe deliberately, excludes aspects of body experiences, of hopelessness and of death." Another gain for her had been that her contributions in the group had helped the family doctors and other specialists in somatic medicine. She was aware though, that her help and advice would probably not be needed in the long term, that her colleagues were well trained to do without her specialist expertise. She expressed her hope that the psychological thinking of the doctor was fortunately well on its way.

I have experienced and firmly believe that Balint work helps to bridge the gap between biological and analytical psychiatry. Psychoanalytical and psychodynamic thinking is introduced into the training of psychiatrists through Balint group work as another pillar in addition to the modern biological approach.

Example 7

A female doctor, in a group of psychiatrists in training, talks about a 49-year-old male patient who had been admitted to hospital for depressive symptoms and was treated pharmacologically.

She has been talking with him regularly and knows his history well. He speaks of things he missed and of his losses. When he was 3 years old his father died in a car accident, his mother was left with five children. His youngest sibling was 8 months old at the time of the father's death; he himself was the second youngest child. The situational demands on his mother were too much to cope with and he quickly learnt to behave in such a way as not to burden her but to help; often he tried to be "invisible". He was still continuing with that behavior and attitude even now. On the ward he was caring and loving and always ready to help. He brought coffee to fellow patients and he listened to their stories; otherwise you hardly noticed him. Three years ago his younger sister committed suicide, his mother died a year ago and, six months prior to admission, his girl-friend of twenty years also committed suicide. Talking to him, the doctor senses that the patient wishes to have a more personal relationship with her. He drops remarks like: "Are you not coming for a swim today?" or "If I had not met you as my doctor..." The doctor is concerned and tells him that they are in a professional doctor–patient relationship and no more than that; but this stance does not seem to have reached him at all. What shocked the doctor most of all is noticing that she feels rather flattered and is tense in their further encounters. In the meantime his condition has improved, he is not depressed any more. The time has come to discharge him from the clinic. She has to prepare for a last consultation, which she would much prefer to avoid, because she dreads it.

The Balint group members know each other well from the group and from working together at the hospital; there is an open and benevolent atmosphere. Problems can be addressed directly and most colleagues show an understanding of the situation. The patient is not that much affected by the depression, he is a nice guy and good looking, he is not demanding, but rather grateful and content with the treatment; he is showing improvement. Most colleagues regard him as comfortable to be with. One female doctor wonders, however, what might have caused the patient's girlfriend to commit suicide, without sharing her problems with him. Why did he not notice that she had been feeling so bad? How might he have behaved in the partnership?

Was he just as caring and considerate as with his fellow patients? Or was there a very different side to him? The presenting doctor now recalled fits of anger on the ward for minor reasons, not often but rather severe; afterwards he had been full of guilty feelings like a little boy. Where had that aggressive side been all along? Had the patient ever used it to grow up and become independent? He often acts in a juvenile, even childish way. The doctor now remembered that he had an alcohol problem. How could she have forgotten about it? A male colleague suggested that she much preferred to see him as a "nice patient" and joined him in the defense of his problems; a collusion in which the patient is pleasant for the doctor and vice versa. He could idealize her. She had time for him whenever he needed her and she provided his medication and gave him support. He could project all his needs for a mother, for a girlfriend and a partner onto her. And he fulfilled the doctor's wish to succeed in helping him and treating his depression. How long might that treatment success last though? Will he be re-admitted soon?

At the end of the group session the doctor says that for now she can let him go. She would have a short and friendly word with him at the last consultation and would be able to cope with a possible readmission with composure. She had found professional distance again, and she was now able to accept the patient with all the sides of his personality, the nice ones and the not so nice, defended ones.

Psychiatrist–patient relationships give plenty of scope for all sorts of entanglements. In talking during therapy, trust develops and a form of professional intimacy can ensue. The treatment is not about a somatic illness or a physical symptom, but about the whole person in his personal and individual situation. Keeping the patient at a distance is neither easy nor desirable. Emotions often flood the relationship in an initially uncontrolled way. The setting on an in-patient ward also fosters regression in the first place and not progression. In that sense the pseudo-autonomous behavior of the presented patient was perceived as pleasant; his improvement was like a present to the treating doctor. But this way a deeper understanding of the underlying dynamic of his depression was not easily possible. In the Balint group a similar process happened initially, with a lot of defensiveness against the "real problem" going on. The advantage of the group setting is that unconscious resonation of the presented situation can often be felt by some group members during the process. In this case, the aggressive side of the patient and his inability to use it for legitimate self-determination was eventually brought up when questioning the motives for the girlfriend's suicide. Contemplations like this take considerable time; that is why we usually allow 90 minutes for one session, analyzing one doctor–patient relationship. When groups start to work, this is often seen as a waste of time. Are there no quicker ways to understand what the problems are? Why does the group leader as an expert not share his psychodynamic knowledge and give some precious explanations? The temptation for the group leader to do so can be rather great. But we know from experience that a rational explanation will get lost soon; whereas an emotional understanding leads to deeper insights and brings about lasting change.

Example 8

A 60-year-old woman has been admitted to the psychiatric clinic with severe fatigue and depression. The female doctor presenting the case in a Balint session shows a great deal of empathy with her situation. The patient is friendly and open, and she soon improves in her mood and energy levels. The doctor knows from taking the history that the patient has been unemployed for a long time. Her husband had been an alcoholic and had died from liver damage; her only son has committed suicide. After those two losses, she had moved back in with her mother and brothers, and, since then, she nursed her mother who is suffering from Alzheimer's disease. Speaking to the patient's brother, a different perspective emerges. He describes her as unreliable and untidy, addicted to buying excessively and taking a considerable amount of medication, mostly analgesics and tranquilizers. At intervals she consumes large amounts of alcohol. The family is more needed in looking after her than she is helpful in nursing her mother. The doctor is indignant and disappointed and feels misled. Ever since the relationship with the patient has been disturbed.

The group members feel the outrage. The patient had been deceiving the doctor: she was dishonest and tried to manipulate the doctor. "A typical addiction patient" is being mentioned. Probably a spoilt child, who is trying to get more attention and is playing one off against the other. Group members speculate how much she has contributed to her own situation, and some wonder how the relationship with her husband and son might have been. Has she been honest there or has she sought center stage there as well? Did she display her depressive symptoms on admission? The presenting doctor now gets irritated when confronted with the group's mood and says she feels ashamed and guilty for painting the picture of her patient in such a bad light. Of course she had been angry, but the patient's depression had been present and she of course would like to help her.

The group recognizes the expressed guilt and shame of the presenter and emotions of the depressed addict as a "parallel process". The members are divided in their reaction: some still continue in empathy with the patient, while others build up a distance and do not wish to be further involved with the woman. The psychiatrist undergoes the back and forth fluctuation with the group members. She is acquainted with these emotions from the encounters with the patient. Now she is able to see that she would like to keep a moderate distance from the patient emotionally, in order to perceive all perspectives clearly and not to turn away completely out of frustration.

Example 9

A student is brought to the psychiatric ward by the police. He had been found naked on a bridge and seemed to be about to jump and commit suicide. He had claimed that his father lay injured in the basement of his house after a violent controversy between the two of them. The police checked the house and found the father well. The student told the doctor on admission that he was fighting for his independence. At the same time, he gave the impression that he was seeking compassion and understanding. The student had been traveling through Europe for the past year in order to distance himself from his family, and had then returned home looking for company and closeness. The young colleague presenting the case says that he understands well what the patient is looking for: closeness without being tied down, a father who respects and accepts him without constant expectations or his own projections. Maybe he had not taken the psychiatric illness seriously enough. That was why he brought the case to the Balint group.

Werner Stucke – psychiatrist and Balint group leader – has often warned of "over-psychologizing" and strongly recommended that psychiatric illness should be diagnosed with the benefit of thorough knowledge. It should be taken seriously and treated properly. A "talking cure" is often not sufficient. Medication may be needed. As an added complication, patients often do not seek help themselves and their treatment is therefore not always strictly voluntary. In this case, the student had been brought to the hospital by the police, and it might have been very difficult to build up sufficient trust and rapport in this situation.

The group members were first dismayed and concerned with the situation: they saw "a poor boy" with a "horrible father", and they felt sorry for him. Some group members became like "big brothers" who wanted to protect him. "Compassion makes small", and the group forgot that the student was an adult in his late 20s. With his adult age recalled and reconsidered, the poor boy "leaves the scene" and a mentally ill adult takes center stage: a man naked on a bridge with an allegedly injured father in the basement. What is behind it? Can this really be explained exclusively in psychodynamic terms? Should the presenter not have considered a psychotic episode? Whatever might have triggered the scene on the bridge, the patient now needed in-patient psychiatric treatment and pharmacological intervention.

As the session develops the doctor is also able to do so. He becomes aware of the identification, into which he has slipped. His feedback to the group is that he has regained his professional position and attitude and is relieved to find that he can now see more clearly.

Chapter 7

Balint work with students

Balint did not initially invite students to take part in his "training cum research" groups; he did not think they were ready to undertake the training in this field of medicine, in psychotherapy:

> On the whole, qualified doctors are much better material for training in psychotherapy than medical students. In the first place, the training is not compulsory; it is not done for examination purposes. Doctors come voluntarily, a self-selected group, who want to acquire a particular new skill because they are interested in it. Secondly, a general practitioner has the inestimable advantage over a medical student of having been knocked about life. He has seen successes and failures, and witnessed a considerable amount of human suffering, which it was his responsibility ... Moreover, a general practitioner is, as a rule, older, more mature, than a medical student. It is questionable whether a young man or woman of twenty or twenty-three years of age, who could hardly have had any real experience of a stable sexual partnership of some duration, who possibly has never earned his living and still less been responsible for a family dependent on him, will be able to understand the subtle and complex ramifications of marital relations and the often profound conflicts between self-centered needs and obligations towards others. In this respect, too, a general practitioner in his late twenties or early thirties is more promising material.
>
> (Balint 1957, p. 297)

Times have changed and so have our experience and our attitude in this respect.

7.1 The Ascona-Balint prize for students

Intensive Balint work with students started in Ascona, Switzerland. In the 1960s Boris Luban-Plozza invited medical students to come to the Monte Vérita (the mountain of truth) above the town. He offered "Junior Balint groups" to talk about the student–patient relationship and made them an important subject of the Ascona meetings. Luban-Plozza invited Michael Balint to take part. He had already convinced him that the groups were useful for the students on a previous occasion when he had demonstrated student Balint groups at a meeting at Milan University.

In 1996 he set up the "Foundation Psychosomatic and Social Medicine". The foundation inaugurated a competition open to medical students from all over the world, with a prize for the best essay on a student–patient relationship, which they experienced and reflected on and from which they had drawn conclusions for the future.

The competition and the Ascona Awards continue. The essays must now be in English. They should describe a student–patient relationship, an experience, or experiences, from the student's medical studies and include critical reflection on personal meetings with patients. The papers should be between 3,000 and 10,000 words.

The criteria by which the papers are judged are as follows:

1. Exposition:
    The paper should include a presentation of a truly personal experience of a student–patient relationship. (Manuscripts of former medical theses or diplomas cannot be accepted.)
2. Reflection:
    A description of how the student experienced this relationship, either individually or as part of the medical team.
3. Action:
    The student's own perception of the demands to which s/he felt exposed and an illustration of how s/he responded.
4. Progression:
    A discussion of ways in which the student's own approach might change in the future, and also possible ways in which future medical training might enhance the state of awareness for individual students.

The Balint prize for students was initially presented yearly in Ascona and is now, since 2003, awarded every second year at the Congress of the International Balint Federation (IBF). The best three essays are selected and the authors are invited to present their papers at the congress. They receive a money prize and all congress expenses are paid for them.

Some of the excellent papers have been published on various occasions (Stubbe and Petzold 1996; Petzold and Otten 2010; Otten and Petzold 2015).

I would like to highlight one of them and give a summarized version.

Example 10

A second year student from Tel Aviv, Israel presented a patient whom he had met in his first year during a course on "medicine in the social context". Students in this course accompany their allocated patient for seven months. During this time they met with him twice per month and participated in group sessions every two to three weeks. Here they discussed their experiences with the other eleven group members and their supervisor. The students' task was to observe how the respective illness influences the patients' psycho-social well-being and to prepare a plan for how the situation could be improved.

The student described how he started the assignment with doubts and anxiety, as he felt he did not have sufficient medical knowledge and experience. His designated patient was a 63-year-old man with back problems, whose mobility was limited despite multiple orthopedic operations. He also suffered from type II diabetes. The patient's general practitioner was also the student's course organizer, who gave the student the additional objective of encouraging the patient to improve his lifestyle, improve his blood sugar regulation and take his medication responsibly. The HbA1c results had been rather poor for a long time, indicating that the diabetes had not been well controlled.

The student visited the patient at home and found that he lived in a friendly and supportive environment with his wife and had good contact with his two children and five grand-children as well as friends and neighbors. After a short while, the student began to enjoy the visits and was looking forward to them. Patient and student liked each other; the patient spoke openly and was willing to answer all the student's questions. Sometimes they talked about politics and sport. The student learned that his patient had been an active sportsman in the past and particularly enjoyed swimming. Ever since his unsuccessful disc operation he had not been able to do sports any more, not even swimming. And he had been avoiding everything which might have been a burden on others. He found it particularly disappointing that his wife now had to fulfill many tasks which had been previously his to do, for example to carry heavy shopping bags. When he talked about it he had tears in his eyes. The adult son also enjoyed swimming and was a voluntary life-guard at the nearby coast. He had supported a disabled wheelchair user regularly and enabled him to go swimming in the sea. The student wondered whether he would not do the same for his father. But his patient replied that the son was too busy in his job and that he did not wish to impinge on his free leisure time. The student raised the question repeatedly. On one occasion towards the end of the seven month course, the patient reported with joy and excitement that his son would shortly pick him up to go swimming. Later the student heard the news that they both had enjoyed it very much, and since then they had been going to the beach together regularly.

When the course was over, the organizer reported back to the student that the HbA1c results had been excellent lately, and she asked him how he had managed to influence the patient. He had to admit that they had never spoken about his diet or medication. He asked himself, what had happened? The patient had changed his lifestyle himself. He had accepted help from his son and both were happy with it. His mood had improved considerably. Had that in itself improved the metabolism? Maybe the patient had followed his doctor's advice more closely, a case of improved compliance or adherence? Certainly the increase of physical exercise must have helped. The student wondered whether he himself had contributed to the positive outcome. He was well aware that later on in his career he would not have that much time and energy to give to all his patients. He also knew that he had not followed the course rules, as he had shaped the relationship in a very personal way and even stayed in contact with the patient after the course had finished. One of the learning objectives had actually been to learn to say goodbye to a patient. Despite these violations of rules, he had learnt a lot about "medicine in a social context". He was now sure that family support must have a positive influence on most aspects of illness as well as that the doctor–patient relationship could really make a great difference.

7.2 Balint group work with students

We found four recurring themes in Balint work with medical students in the last year before graduation from university:

a. problems the students are having in their own socialization during medical training
b. the role of the student during his practical year at the university hospital
c. confrontation with the ideal image of being a doctor and the reality
d. the wish and need for self-experience

When students report about their student–patient relationship, there are often underlying institutional and hierarchical factors. This raises an important question: "How do those factors possibly influence the relationship with patients?" A further look reveals the importance of systems and their influence on dual relationships.

Leading student groups has some special features. The doctor or psychologist leading is often perceived either as representative of the clinic and the medical establishment or as an opponent of the simply rational side of somatic medicine. Sometimes he is idealized as the doctor, who is aware of his own emotional reactions and possibilities; at the same time he takes good care of the patient's physical and his emotional concerns with a holistic view.

In the Balint group, students deal with their struggle with everyday facts in clinical work, which they experience as insufficient and annoying. After a while they become more tolerant, realistic and get a more differentiated picture of an idealistic and a feasible approach to the patient, while the focus is on both sides: the rational and the emotional, the somatic and the psychological.

Students in Balint groups often describe their difficulties of being in tune with the patient and keeping professional distance at the same time. During their training they get advice and rules or guidance but find it difficult to keep the rules and act accordingly.

Example 11

A male student confesses to his group that he had given his phone number to a young and attractive female patient, despite being aware that this felt wrong and unprofessional immediately afterwards. The patient was a student of biology, and she had attended the emergency room for examination of lower abdominal pain. It had been the medical student's job to take a history. He asked the necessary questions and she answered in a friendly and open manner; afterwards they chatted for a while. Then he turned to the next patient. Some time was left when he had finished his duties and he decided to do some extra ultrasound scans for practice.

When he entered the examination room, this young woman lay naked on the couch. He was surprised and his heart was racing, but he tried to be professional and performed the examination. He returned to a chatting mode, and, while saying goodbye, he asked whether they could meet sometime again and gave her his telephone number. Afterwards he felt that he had made a mistake. He immediately discussed the matter with his registrar, who debriefed and reassured him, but he still felt very bad.

He presented the case with feelings of guilt, shame and discomfort. He expected to be reprimanded by the group for his unprofessional conduct: "How could you ever do this...?" But to the contrary, almost every group member had a similar story to tell. The theme of the group was emotional participation, closeness and proximity and the difficulty of setting boundaries. Students are in a difficult role and position, not quite doctors yet but no longer just ordinary citizens in a helping position. They feel uncertain about their role with regard to the patients, whose expectations are not clear to them. And the students are aware that they still have a lot to learn.

The Balint group, while not meant to be a support group as such, can at least give room for reflection, sharing of experiences and clarification of issues.

The student Balint group can bring emotional relief through sharing problems with others and give orientation. In comparison with doctors' groups, their self-experience is more pronounced. The situations described by the students are mostly emotionally challenging, sometimes overwhelming. Uncertainty in their professional and learning role leads to the experience of helplessness and dependency. With those emotions, the students are close to the patients. In mixed groups together with senior doctors, students indeed tend to take the patient's or their relative's perspective. Thus they are sensitized to reflect about relationship experiences.

While the focus in medical training may well be on aspects of academic medicine, clinical as well as somatic realities, the students also become interested in the meaning of interaction and the psychological background.

As demonstrated in example 10, psychosomatic questions arise: "Is it possible that the biochemical metabolism is influenced by psychological factors, by the mental condition of the patient?"

Students mostly are very open towards psychosomatic views. It coincides with their primary professional interest. Many of them start their medical studies with the ideal of holistic medicine. The social orientation prevails; the aim is to help and to heal. During medical school the interest shifts to the more scientific contents and the psycho-social orientation fades into the background. Patients are seen as "cases" and "symptom carriers". The doctor–patient relationship and its importance for diagnosis and treatment is not mentioned. Junior Balint groups filled this gap. Nowadays we find Balint groups in medical schools – integrated in the curriculum – in many countries.

Example 12

A female student is doing her placement in the obstetric department of a university hospital. She is seeing a young couple, both also students, who are expecting their first child. The student is allowed to stay in the delivery suite when the child is born. As the birth progresses through its stages she notices the delivery team "holding their breath" and becoming tense. She looks at the baby and clearly sees that there is something wrong with it; most likely this child has a genetic defect – Down's syndrome. The young mother asks whether everything is okay with the child, but no one seems to be ready to answer. Eventually someone replies: "Yes, the pediatrician will have a look at the child soon, just a matter of routine." Everyone quickly leaves the room when the specialist enters, but the student stays. The pediatrician also looks concerned when examining the baby. He mentions that he wants to consult his registrar and then also leaves. Now the student stays alone with the newborn and the young mother who by this time has become anxious. The student would have preferred to talk openly to her, but follows instructions to leave the diagnosis and explanations to the qualified doctors. It takes a long time until the registrar arrives which the student finds difficult to bear. After another examination, the registrar conveys his findings in a factual and somewhat distanced way and leaves; the student senses his unease. The patient seems rather composed and is grateful for the student being with her. The student feels like crying, not up to the situation, left alone and abandoned. She is angry that nobody is looking after the young mother and that she has not been told what is going to happen from now on.

The group is also embarrassed: "I would not like to be treated this way." The students empathize with the patient and the student. They find it difficult to take the perspective of the experienced obstetrician and pediatrician. They understand that nobody likes to be the bearer of bad news, but should that not be a very important part of medical training? How would they in the mother's shoes wish to be supported? Some of the professionals should take the time to sit at the bedside and explain the situation in a calm, understanding, empathetic way. The doctor should answer the mother's questions, share the mourning and the pain of the patient, and not run away. Giving birth to a disabled child means saying goodbye to the image of the expected healthy child and welcoming this other newborn who will usher in a different life perspective for the parents.

This report and group discussion will stay in their minds and will be recalled when these students become qualified responsible doctors. From the beginning, Balint work for students makes sense.

Mixed groups bring doctors and students together and both can learn a lot from each other. We cannot share Balint's early concerns about their lack of age, wisdom and life experience. Students enrich the discussion with their actual view on life and their coping strategies. They are spontaneous and empathic, open and curious and thus they vitalize the group work. And they receive a back-stage view of the working life of experienced colleagues, their conflicts, insecurities, dilemmas and burdens, not normally openly shared in the day to day running of a hospital ward.

7.3 The UCL Student Psychotherapy Scheme

The University College of London developed and practiced for the last thirty years a very interesting teaching approach to help medical students understand the role of emotions in illness, communicate more effectively and gain a deeper understanding of the doctor–patient relationship (Shoenberg and Yakeley 2014). Students are offered the possibility of learning from and reflecting on a real experience with a patient in psychodynamic psychotherapy for one year. The students are closely accompanied by experienced supervisors in a group of peers. Thus they learn directly about patients' emotions, as well as to better appreciate their own emotional responses to illness and to communicate better with their patients. Further experienced Balint group leaders, such as Peter Shoenberg and Heather Suckling, offer short-term student Balint discussion groups to provide clear guidance about how psychotherapeutic understanding can be used to support medical education. The idea is to give the students a safe setting to reflect about the patients' and their own emotions. If the strong feelings evoked by the student–patient encounters are not reflected the students often develop – as investigations show – resistance strategies like a cool distance to patients or cynicism. The Student Psychotherapy Scheme is an attempt to contribute to revive the emotional access to the unwell human being: from "illness-centered medicine" to "patient-centered medicine".

Chapter 8

Homogeneous and heterogeneous Balint groups

Balint started with a homogeneous group of general medical practitioners and set out to research the drug "doctor". Today's groups mostly emphasize training, learning and experience. Balint work is now part of postgraduate training for doctors, psychologists and psychotherapists and focuses on analytic thinking, psychosomatic medicine and psychodynamics. Reflecting on difficult interactions, the group members find relief. They are able to understand their own experiences in forming relationships, and by changing perspectives, the shared experiences of the others.

A homogeneous group consists of, for example, only general practitioners, exclusively gynecologist psychiatrists or psychologists. The participants share basic premises, common ground and similar experiences in their everyday working lives and structures. Relatively little has to be explained and understanding and empathy come more easily. The disadvantage may well be that all group members are handicapped by by the same "blind spots", which usually come up in Balint work: they do not question what they take for granted.

Balint as a psychiatrist tried to compensate for the lack of insight by stimulating a change of perspective in his group with GPs. His co-leader, his wife Enid, with the benefit of her social work training was able to contribute a different point of view. In their groups, they were less "abstinent" and more active. Explanations were given, and their own insights and experiences shared. However, Balint was aware of the danger of becoming the "smartest group member" (Balint 1957) instead of taking care of his original tasks as a group leader.

In heterogeneous groups the members may come from different professional backgrounds besides embodying religious, cultural and gender diversity. In such groups, reports and backgrounds have to be explained in more detail: terminology, diagnostic methods and therapy need to be clarified for everybody. Another big advantage of these groups is that prejudices are exposed and reviewed. It may take longer for these groups to achieve group coherence and educational alliance, but the horizon is wide and the work intense.

Kornelia Rappe-Giesecke (2000) describes the advantages of homogeneous and heterogeneous groups. In homogeneous groups, many issues can be introduced and do not have to be explained, for example, terminology or operation methods or examination techniques. A group of gynecologists can be certain that they have a similar basic knowledge regarding, for example, the method and difficulties of artificial insemination.

When participants come from different backgrounds, explanations and elaboration will often be necessary. The clarifying questions can already lead the presenter to rethink his case and submit a modified request to the group. When a heterogeneous group starts associating, the members often bring up very different fantasies, pictures and perceptions from "different worlds" – from different occupational areas and other social backgrounds. A social worker experiences the operation theater differently from the surgeon; a pastor has a different view of the psychiatric clinic than a psychiatrist. An exchange of thoughts from these different perspectives and the emotions related to them is very illuminating.

8.1 Various professional groups

Heterogeneous can thus mean that doctors from different specialties work together in the same group. It can also refer to groups in which helpers from different occupations are gathered, like students, physicians, psychologists, nurses, social workers, ergotherapists, medical assistants, physiotherapists, music therapists, hospital chaplains and teachers. The pre-condition and understanding in those groups is that every participant is willing to be truly involved in the clarifying process and to contribute stories of their own difficult relationships. Another very important condition is confidentiality: everything that is said in the group stays in the group and is not discussed elsewhere.

Example 13

A female hospital chaplain speaks about a female in-patient, who has consulted her repeatedly over the recent past. In these consultations the pastor offered an opportunity to the patients of the psychiatric ward to discuss their questions of faith. This particular patient feels abandoned by God and vulnerable as well as unprotected in the daily busy reality of the hospital. She perceives the doctors and nurses on her ward in the same way, as not caring for her enough and as not listening. She feels that her carers have subordinated themselves to the economic pressures and to the power of the hospital management. The pastor empathizes with this sentiment, because she has a similar perception of the clinic structures. We create a sculpture together in the group (Chapter 9, section 9.1). The presenter sets the following picture: the patient lies on the carpet with the pastor kneeling right next to her; standing and looking down on them are the doctor and a male and a female nurse. She places the hospital management standing on a chair above the rest. In the interview of the protagonists we learn that all the people involved feel uncomfortable in their position; even the adminis-tration department feels lonely and insecure, despite looking down on everyone from their height. In the second sculpture, which is set by the protagonist of the patient, everyone involved is on the same eye level, an unfamiliar experience. Now the patient feels insecure, the manage-ment is much more capable of acting and the protagonist of the pastor would now like to leave the group together with the patient.

At first the group discussed the patient's mental illness, which stayed vague in the presenter's report, in the sculpture and in her perception. The psychiatrists, especially, wanted to know more about it. What changes in the perception if the patient is no longer seen as a victim of the institution, but rather as suffering from an illness? Who is to blame for her fate? Do we not all try to find someone to blame? The patient initially takes her frustration to the pastor and complains that there is no longer a loving God who protects her and can be relied upon, who refuses to leave her alone unlike the doctors and nurses. Both patient and pastor find it a relief that they can put the blame on the "evil admin" and unburden God. The first sculpture depicts the hierarchy as rigid and non-negotiable with the patient at the very bottom and only the pastor kneeling almost at her level, facing and supporting her. The ones holding the power do not care in that first picture. The desire of the patient for all to be equal leads to the second sculpture. But, surprisingly, the patient does not feel good in this constellation either. And the pastor wishes to escape the hospital together with the patient in order to save her. At this point it is not only the psychiatrists who question whether a move like that would take the severe illness of the patient into account, whether it would help the patient. Was the pastor seduced by the patient into contemplating this seemingly easy solution? Is this not the idea, that "I would be healthy if everybody treated me right"?

Illness is insulting and mental illness even more so. Joint denial and defense relieves and liberates in the first place. It does not however lead to adequate treatment; the lack of acceptance might indeed make helpful treatment impossible. What does the patient really need?

The pastor left the group in deep thought and contemplation.

She had started the group in judgment and anger about the conditions in the psychiatric clinic, then she became rather ashamed not to have taken the psychiatric illness into account properly. Finally she was relieved to conclude that views and positions can be changed and corrected much more easily, when communication with other specialists is possible: "I should maintain contact with my colleagues of different specializations, and communicate more, before identifying or showing solidarity with my patients – maybe in mutual denial and defense and not to their benefit."

This group was an impressive demonstration, also for the other group members, the social workers, doctors and psychologists. Are we not all easily tempted to deny reality, to look for somebody to blame, to make the system responsible, at least the others in the system, which we are no doubt part of? And can it not also be just as misleading to create projection sites and illusions? "It would be possible if only...", "everyone would be better off if...". In the end the group realized that feelings of impotence and helplessness towards an illness and the associated anger are often projected and defended against.

The different perspectives introduced by group members from their real experiences in their field made a substantial contribution to the clarification and enlightenment.

8.2 Different cultural backgrounds and nationalities

Another form of heterogeneous group is the one consisting of participants from different cultures and different countries. Naturally we find this setting at the International Congresses, but also increasingly at other institutions or when doctors meet locally in their regional groups, to acquire skills and certificates in "psychosomatic basic care". Without doubt any form of cross-cultural exchange is enriching, not only since we, as doctors, are looking after patients from more than one cultural background. Recently at a weekend seminar we met group members from India, Pakistan, Turkey, Poland, Vietnam and Germany.

Example 14

A German colleague presents a patient who grew up in a mountainous border region of Afghanistan, fled to Turkey with his family and came to Germany as an adolescent. Now he was an in-patient on a psychiatric ward being treated for depression. The doctor wanted to find out in the group, what kind of help he could offer. He found it difficult to engage, since the patient was not able to express his problems nor share his experiences. The doctor was also not sure regarding his own emotions towards the patient, who he knew had killed others in order to survive. He felt uneasy in the patient's presence. On the other hand he was ashamed. He had been brought up under safe conditions and never experienced heavy suffering or life-threatening events in his childhood or youth. He wanted to mention and talk about the injustice, which that contrast entailed.

Example 15

At the same weekend workshop another female doctor shared the story of a female patient, who had been living in former Yugoslavia; she had moved to Germany ten years ago. Her German was still very poor; the 16-year-old daughter had to act as her interpreter. The doctor found out that the patient was beaten by her husband, and her oldest son had returned to former Yugoslavia because he had broken the law in Germany. Her second son did not get along with the father and therefore had completely withdrawn from the family. The woman had tried to leave her husband with the support of her daughter, but she had failed to actually separate. Now she felt safe being treated in hospital. The doctor perceives her patient as suicidal and feels she cannot be discharged. She does not see the husband open for any meaningful communication.

What do we understand from each other, deriving from backgrounds we never had access to?

Can we truly empathize with a patient, a refugee who had to escape twice from dangerous situations, who lost his roots completely, worked for the secret service and may have killed others? What is the aim of our treatment? Can German psychiatry help, can medication and can the therapist?

Do we understand the structure and dynamics of the Yugoslavian family, their experiences and their past? Is the patient in the right place in a psychiatric hospital in Germany? There seems to be no change in the patient's mood or condition and none in the outer circumstances. What sort of relationship can be built between doctor and patient despite the language barriers?

The group is international and tries to empathize. Own experiences are willingly shared. Are we really getting closer to the patient?

The themes of this weekend workshop mirror facts and problems in society as such and raise questions about integration, tolerance and empathy. There are anxieties, defenses and misunderstandings.

The group is trying hard to understand what health and healing would mean in the two cases. Is the violent husband the root of all evil or is it home-sickness or sadness about the son who went away, the falling apart of the family? Every group member has his own fantasies, according to his background.

Can the depressive patient from Afghanistan reflect and draw a line under his past life, can he start afresh? Is this possible in a strange country, where he does not feel at home?

And yet we experience during the weekend that a common understanding of the emotions is possible. Sharing empathy and understanding skips barriers.

No matter what background, cultural origin and past experiences we have, an interpersonal relationship is possible, mostly so on an emotional level including loneliness and approach, acceptance and rejection.

At this internationally composed Balint seminar we used roleplay, imagination, sculpturing and psychodrama. The pictures that were painted left little room for misunderstanding. Those pictures gave an immediate emotional impact. During group work at a later stage we carefully attempted to transcribe pictures and emotions into words and language.

8.3 Balint work in different countries

The International Balint Congresses are characterized by the mixed groups with participants from different countries and cultural origins. The exchange in these groups is an enrichment and helps us understand cultures, ethical demands, health care systems, political and social backgrounds and their influence on the professional relationships.

Example 16

In Croatia, a family doctor speaks of a woman whom he has been treating for many years. Their last encounter had rendered him helpless and sad. It was the time shortly after the war (War in Croatia 1991–1995). The patient came to his consultation and he briefly welcomed her in the corridor. There were a few more patients before it was her turn; she sat down in the waiting room. When the doctor called her, she was not there, she had left. After a while her husband showed up and explained what had happened. His wife had watched the doctor shaking hands with a Serb and had had to run away. The husband begged his pardon, his wife had experienced terrible things during the war. She had been raped by a Serbian man, and he describes that it would be impossible for her to be examined bodily by the doctor, whose hand had touched the hand of a Serb. She felt very sorry, claimed that she always had great trust and respect for the doctor and still has, but she could not bear the situation. The doctor is very affected. He could understand the patient's feelings, but on the other hand he was determined not to make any difference in the treatment and acceptance of patients from different ethnic groups now, just as it had been before the war.

The group members, coming from different countries and cultures, feel initially helpless. The sadness spreads. They express empathy with the patient and with the doctor. Will time heal the wounds? Is there anybody to offer trauma therapy to the woman? There are so many traumatized people after a war. And what about the doctor himself, who has also experienced the war? He had mentioned that his own children had been more capable of identifying war planes by the particular sound they make, than the bird song in their garden. He had been afraid when his children were on their way to school. He is able to speak about his worries, the patient could not. Maybe one day? There is some hope, she might need time. How much time? Memories are shared from other countries, from other post-war situations: a patient in Germany left her doctor's waiting room when a Polish visitor entered, who now lived in the place which she had to leave during the war seventy years ago. She also had experienced bad things as a young woman and obviously has not processed these experiences since then.

The presenting doctor has a good and long relationship with his patient and he likes her; she does not accuse him or hold him responsible. He wants to help her and will leave his door open for her.

Example 17

At a Balint workshop in Romania a female colleague shared about her experience with a family. Mother and son are both being treated for high blood pressure. She does not see much of either of them, they mainly collect their prescriptions. The mother's blood pressure was initially very high and difficult to control. The son's diagnosis had been somewhat vague and she felt he was afraid to follow his mother's hypertensive path. When she told him one day that he would not need anti-hypertensive medication any longer, he became nervous and sad. When further questioned, he admitted that he never took his medication himself, but had given the pills to his mother as a top-up. The doctor told the group that medication supply in Romania was rationed and she had indeed been unable to prescribe medication to the mother in sufficient amounts. The old lady indeed had a sufficient treatment only with her son's medication. Now she, the doctor, faced the difficulty of deciding whether to support this fraudulent transaction or not. Should she continue to prescribe medication to the son, which he did not need and did not use? What would happen if she decided not to? Would the patient die from a stroke or a heart attack one day? And what would happen to herself if her cheating was found out? Would she be punished, lose her job?

This was a difficult situation. Group members were outraged about the health care system, which would not supply the patients with sufficient medication. Others were relieved to be privileged enough, not having to work in such circumstances, although some rationing already existed in almost every country and the worry was there, that it could become much worse because of the age pyramid and the increasing expenses in health systems all over.

The son's action was seen as honorable rather than fraudulent. He had nevertheless maneuvered the family doctor into a difficult situation. Could he not have kept it for himself and found a better explanation for still needing his medication? Solidarity became a theme in the group; should wealthier countries not support the poorer ones more effectively? Was there a difference between absolutely necessary treatments and more debatable or even luxurious ones, or was there not? Was the problem here a global one or could it only be approached on an individual level? Various problems were raised and many constructive ideas followed, well aware that the conflict of the presenter could not be solved by the group. She had to make her own decision. Hopefully the discussion had been a support.

Chapter 9

Balint groups with added creative elements

Balint work is practiced to enable the presenting group member to gain a different perspective on the shared doctor–patient relationship and to learn about the influences on this relationship by his own personality, by the environment and by the system they live and work in.

This is achieved through free associations, fantasies and pictures arising in the group process.

Access to emotions and fantasies can be improved by combining the analytical approach with other, well-known, tried and tested psychotherapeutic methods.

The question has been put as to "whether this is still Balint", whether adding methods taken from systemic therapy – like the sculpturing – from psychodrama, role-play or imagination techniques harm or enrich Balint work.

Philipp Herzog (2016) recently published an article in the *German Balint Journal*, where he answers this question with "yes" and "no".

It may not be Balint in the original version; although when you follow the transcripts of Balint's first group sessions, you would not say that today's structured "classical" Balint group work is the same. And the methods of psychotherapy and psychoanalysis have changed over time, too. Philipp reminds us that Balint himself contributed to the development of psychoanalysis with his ideas of the object-relation theory. Following this aspect Balint work deals with the doctor–patient relationship instead of focusing on the inner world and dynamics of the patient only.

Balint work is characterized by the "think fresh" impulse, by openness, tolerance and respect for the ideas of others. Why should Balint have anything against experimenting with creative elements and new experiences? Having witnessed the "Horty" regime in Hungary and two World Wars, he himself was interested in the influence social and political realities had on the patient, on the doctor and on the doctor–patient relationship. Maybe sculpturing would have fascinated him. He was open for fresh impulses. He called his group a "training cum research group" to constantly question his hypothesis and findings. In the first place he was skeptical about students as participants, later on he was leading student groups in Ascona with pleasure. He was skeptical about psychiatrists reflecting about their patient relationship. He revised this, too.

Introducing a new method means that there was the impression that in classical Balint groups some aspects are missing, that the rich emotional content and background of the professional relationship might be experienced more deeply in a different setting. And those pictures seen in a sculpture or role-play stay and can be recalled long after. So let us not deny it, but think about pro and contra.

9.1 Sculpture

One of the methods, known from the systemic approach, is that of creating a sculpture. The method was developed in family therapy by Virginia Satir in the 1970s. Thea Schönfelder demonstrated the method impressively in the 1980s in Lübeck at the Northern German Psychotherapy week.

Through sculpturing the presenting therapist operates with the possibility to make difficult relationships visible by members of the group and thus gets new ideas, impressions and draws his conclusions. The protagonists are representing people or institutions, even concepts or symptoms which play a part in the difficult relationship being explored.

While the group members are representing the "figures" involved in the problematic relationship as part of the sculpture, the presenter is given the chance to look at his problem and himself being represented by somebody else, too, from a distance.

This distance can help him to see more clearly, discover blind spots and gain new impressions; the quality of affect and emotion will change.

And this is how it works: like in every other Balint session, the presenter shares the case history, which is followed by factual questions and answers. The leader then asks the presenter to name all the people and parties which are involved in the situation or might have a bearing influence. On the side of the doctor these could be the consultant or registrars, nurses, the hospital administration, receptionist, the health insurance or public health system and others. On the patient's side he may name relatives, colleagues, friends, superiors at work and the illness. In other professional relationships you will find equal representatives. Now the presenter looks for protagonists in the group and places them. It is important to find the adequate matching distance, the line of sight and posture for each single representative. The group leader assists the presenter to form the sculpture without influencing his work.

The sculptor may take his time, can reconsider and reposition and should have a look at the sculpture from all angles. The group members watch attentively, register their observations, feelings and perceptions and will later on in the group discussion share them with the presenter.

When the installation is finished, the sculptor steps behind each figure and gives him one sentence to emphasize the role.

Then he steps back, the figures remain in their allocated position for quite a while, remember their given sentence and concentrate on their emotional reactions.

The group leader now interviews everyone in the sculpture about their feelings and thoughts in an order which is determined by the presenter. Again, the group members could make important observations: has someone been left out, maybe the presenter himself or the patient? Who is interviewed first and who last?

The figures are also asked to make suggestions and share their wishes for a better position in the picture: would they for example like to change their own or somebody else's position or posture? Do they need to be closer or further away from someone else? Would they like to take someone else's hand or free themselves from a weight, etc.?

The presenter listens carefully to all offers and then allows somebody to change his sculpture, which was his inner picture of the situation. Afterwards every figure in this new constellation is again interviewed by the group leader and shares the different feelings and thoughts, again in a sequence decided by the sculptor.

Because of the time structure the leader may allow only one or maximum two changes. That normally provides the group with enough material for the subsequent group discussion.

Just prior to the following discussion the figures are actively released from their position by the presenter and go back into the Balint group circle.

I recently learned from Vladimir Vinokur in a Balint workshop in Moscow to ask the presenter right after whether his request to the group might have changed while watching the sculpture. This is an excellent idea to come back to the original analytic Balint work.

Then the group leader – luckily it is the co-leader – is free to process the group. He may involve the observers first who were not actually part of the sculpture, to share their thoughts. This way the protagonists have the chance to distance more from their role and come back to being a group member. Everybody now has the chance to contribute, no matter whether it is an observation going back to the report or to setting the scene or the interviews. New pictures, emotions and thoughts may have been triggered. Finally – as usual – the focus moves to the doctor–patient relationship considering the influencing factors.

Summarizing the structure of the group process:

1. the presenter describes the case in free form
2. short questions for clarification
3. the presenter names all persons and facts which he thinks have an influence on the relationship
4. he chooses the protagonists from the group
5. he positions the figures creating a sculpture, assisted by the group leader
6. the presenter gives every person one sentence describing his feelings
7. the protagonists take time to concentrate on the role and their emotional reactions
8. the group leader interviews everyone in the sculpture in an order determined by the presenter
9. calls for change are registered
10. the presenter allows one or two figures to change the sculpture according to their wishes
11. a new sculpture emerges
12. the protagonists are interviewed again in their new position
13. the presenter releases the participants from their roles
14. the following group discussion will be taken on by the co-leader if possible. He may start by asking the presenter whether his request has changed, and then invite the observers to comment
15. group work as usual continues with all group members
16. the presenter shares his feelings and insights

The presenter navigates through the following phases during his presentation:

1. report on the relationship
2. answering factual questions
3. choice of important people and facts influencing the relationship
4. choice of representatives out of the group members
5. building the sculpture
6. giving one sentence to every figure
7. observing from a distance
8. deciding in which order participants would be interviewed by the group leader
9. listening attentively to the interviews and keeping in mind the wishes for change of posture and positioning
10. choice of who may change the sculpture
11. choice of the order for the second interviews
12. reflecting and then communicating whether the request to the group has changed
13. push-back and attentive listening to the following group discussion
14. final expression of own insights and possibly changed emotions relating to the presented patient

When observing the sculpture, it often happens that the presenter realizes how he and the patient are positioned to each other, how their relationship seems to be for him. Surely it is his perception, his inner picture of the patient and his choice of actors and their positioning.

The group discussion never changes reality, but it will most likely change the inner picture of the protagonist. In that sense we are encouraging a changing point of view and felt relationship.

Example 18

A female general practitioner presents a 79-year-old woman, whom she visits regularly at her home. The patient has been bed bound since a certain time and is cared for by her family. When the doctor visits, there are always numerous people in the room, she has never been able to speak to the patient separately. Mostly a family member answers the doctor's question: "How have you been last week?" The daughter answers: "Oh, grandma had back pain again. We would have liked her to sit on the chair, but she refuses." Doctor: "I would like to examine your back." The patient is about to turn around and pull up her

night-shirt. Granddaughter: "Wait grandma, leave it, I will help you."
The doctor feels anger arising in herself, but at the same time she is
quite touched by the caring attitude of the 15-year-old granddaughter.
When she proceeds with her examination, no one leaves or steps aside.
The patient is completely passive. "She could do much more if one lets
her", the doctor tells the group. She reflects that she did not have the
courage to mention this to the family.

The scene around the patient's bed is reconstructed in the sculpture.
The protagonist for the patient lies on a table, very closely surrounded
by two daughters, one granddaughter, a nurse who visits daily and the
doctor. All of them are leaning forward towards the patient reaching
out for her. When interviewed, the patient expresses how pressed she
feels, so that she can hardly breathe. The family members feel helpless
and exhausted in their position. The female nurse is angry and feels
redundant and the doctor experiences competition. The presenter
allows the patient to change according to her voiced needs: everyone
moves five steps back, only the nurse stays close and lifts the patient's
leg as if helping with the daily hygiene. At the second interview everyone feels relieved: the relatives are more relaxed and not that much
bound to duty; the nurse can do her job now and is in good contact
with the patient, the doctor found her role again as the professional
adviser when needed and the uncomfortable feeling of competition
is gone. And the patient can breathe easily now; she is content to be
alone with her nurse.

The following group discussion showed disparity between doctor and relatives concerning the needs of the patient. The doctor
wants to obtain as much autonomy as possible for her patient, but
had never asked the patient yet what she would like for herself. The
family is committed to do everything for grandmother, to care for
her in the best way, but they also did not question her needs. And
the patient apparently fears losing care and help, if she would voice
her wishes and show her potential for more autonomy. The group
pointed out as noteworthy that the presenter asked the patient
to change the sculpture. She obviously had gotten an important
impression already from the first setting: that the patient was able
and powerful enough to make the change with confidence and a
little support.

The pictures stay, as much with the presenter as with the group
members, protagonists and observers. The patient lying in bed surrounded by family and helpers will be remembered. And for the

protagonists the accompanying emotions will be retrievable: the patient not being able to breathe, the helpers competing, the family members being helpless and anxious. Experiencing a role is different from talking about it.

A surprising aspect of sculpturing is that matters are felt and expressed which the presenter has not mentioned. Often the actors slip into their roles very comfortably and identify without difficulty; they get some self-experience out of it. And the acted change of perspective becoming the patient, the nurse or the granddaughter – maybe in another sculpture the head of the clinic or the management director – expands our horizon effectively.

The effects of perspective change naturally potentiate. Every group member knows similar situations, patients and relationships. Being part of a sculpture, feeling it unfold, empathizing and questioning own patterns is self-experience everyone takes home. In the Balint group we do not discuss the self-experience aspects.

To introduce the sculpture into Balint work depends on the leader's personality, his ability and tendency to integrate a more "playful" method. And he has to be familiar with systemic group work.

As well, the group members have to be ready for the experiment to work with such a technique, which they might not know. It is important to explain it with all its background information beforehand. The sculpture is experienced as emotionally sophisticated and demanding, and thus exhausting.

The aim of Balint work after all is to work for the presenter; his requests are in the center. He has to be protected on one hand; on the other hand his blind spots should be enlightened with fresh fantasies, ideas and pictures, no matter which method we use or add.

9.2 Role-play

Role-play is another creative element which we can integrate into the process of a Balint session.

A group member presents his encounter with a patient, factual questions can be asked and group members then share their thoughts and feelings as usual. Sometimes within the discussion a role-play sequence may appear. Two colleagues identify with different persons in the story – and suddenly they talk to each other alike. This is an advantage for the group leader, who just has to point out what is going on, and use it for the further discussion.

In case he wants to invent a role-play for better understanding and emotional access the leader will ask the presenter to play the role of the patient and another group member to take his – the doctor's – part. They replay a situation and a dialogue which has taken place during the consultation. When the presenter slips into the patient's shoes, he feels the potency of the words which he had used in the real situation. Different group members then may play and you can feel the nuances and differences. This way you become well aware of what transference and counter-transference mean.

Example 19

A female general practitioner presents a 23-year-old woman, who had consulted her frequently in the recent past with pain in various parts of her body. At present her main concern is chest pain, prior to that it was a cramping pain in her lower abdomen. So far the doctor had patiently and thoroughly examined her repeatedly, but had not found any physical reason for the pains.

It had been difficult talking to the patient, since her responses had been sparse. She works as a sales assistant, which she does not like very much. She still lives with her parents, which she did not choose voluntarily; she had not been able to keep her apartment after her boy-friend had left and moved out. "But that has nothing to do with my pain. Why do you want to know all this?" The doctor tries to answer, but feels her anger and frustration. She is stuck with the patient.

We integrate a sequence of role-play. The doctor demonstrates how the patient sits in front of her, head down, a little bit overweight, tidy but dressed with no great care in jeans and a white T-shirt. Dark blond hair hanging down to her shoulders, she seems to be without energy. A male colleague takes the part of the doctor, repeats the questions regarding work and her relationship and receives monosyllabic answers. He feels frustrated and would love to send the patient home, but without a sick leave, as he stresses. Another female group member tries to reach her with speculations: "I can imagine that you would like a more satisfying job and to move into your own flat again." "That would not work anyway, my pains are so strong, I cannot do anything anyhow", replies the presenter in the role of the patient.

Another group member has the idea to say to her: "I think it must have been very difficult to move back to one's parents. On one side it may be nice to be cared for and having fewer expenses, but on the other side I would hate to have to follow regulations again what to do and what not to do." That touches something in the patient. "Yes you are right", says the presenter in the place of the patient. The group discussion shows that this group member has met the focus, her conflict; a young ambivalent woman between autonomy and dependence, who had detached and then went back home. The presenter now realizes that by looking after the patient she would support further regression. That is what she definitely does not want to do.

She now describes her counter-transference as being the big sister of the patient, who as the little sister has resettled with her parents, feels she wants to push her out, metaphorically speaking give her a good kick. She can laugh about it now and her anger has disappeared. She is looking forward to the next meeting with the patient and is confident of being better prepared to find some new angle and ideas.

The role-play showed in a very short time what was really going on in this relationship. The group dived into the emotions of both protagonists. And demonstrating the situation led to the underlying conflict; transference and counter-transference became clear and could be named.

9.3 Psychodrama

Psychodrama is extended role-play, developed by Moreno. Balint work and Moreno's idea of being creative by improvising fit well together. Moreno's concept of spontaneity explains the Balint group dynamics as well:

Spontaneity drives the individual towards adequate reactions to new situations or towards new reactions to an old situation.

(Moreno 1974, p. 13)

Precondition for change in relationships is the growth in the premier quality to act in a way, which is necessary for breaking up fixations. ... the spontaneous person acts as if he was a beginner. Every moment is new.

(Krüger 1997, p. 16)

This matches Balint's demand "to think fresh". He expects the group members to engage in the situation, to focus on the feelings of the moment and to fully concentrate on the story presented.

In psychodrama a scene from the doctor–patient relationship is reconstructed in all its details: what does the consulting room look like, in which the patient enters? Where does the view of the doctor go to and where does the patient look? What do they sense and experience in the room? What energies, what feelings are present? One can feel the energy and tension in the encounter. The protagonist plays himself and chooses a group member for the patient. He dives into the moment when he met with the problematic patient, which he now brings to the Balint group.

Example 20

A family physician tells the story of a 65-year-old woman complaining about gall bladder problems. He saw her for the first time. He soon realized he was becoming impatient when listening to her descriptions and complaints. He wishes her to leave the consultation quickly, but also feels guilty because the patient might have noticed his difficulty to tolerate her. He had sent her for laboratory tests before she stopped talking. He feels uncomfortable anticipating the next consultation, which is scheduled for the next week to discuss findings and results.

The group leader asks him to reconstruct his consulting room: door, windows, desk, chairs and other furniture. The desk is in the middle of the room, a swinging chair in front for him, on the right hand side the patient's chair. Left of the desk there is a window, behind his chair there are book-shelves with books, pictures and small objects. The view of the doctor goes straight towards the door. He replays the scene: the patient enters the room together with the receptionist, he shakes her hand, invites her to sit down in the patient's chair and turns to her to listen. She then starts to describe her complaints.

The group leader and the other group members are outside the scene. They are allowed to "double up" when they feel that unspoken preconscious thoughts are present in the room. The presenter says to the patient: "How are you? What brings you here?" A group member doubles what he may sense: "Actually I do not really want to know; I already see that she is unhappy with everything in her life." Even in this short scene the observers feel the tension.

The group leader notices that the doctor mostly does not look at the patient who speaks of her problems, but at the book-shelf behind her. He interrupts the scene and asks: "What is on the shelf there?" The doctor pauses for thought and responds: "The picture of my father." At that moment he realizes whom he is seeing in the patient and why he anticipates what she will say, how unhappy she is with her life. And he understands his emotional reaction: his subliminal anger, his impatience, his desire to make her leave as soon as possible.

The group learns how his transference had influenced the relationship from the beginning.

The self-experience part is not discussed further. As soon as the presenter knows whom he had seen in the patient, he is free to notice other aspects in her. After all she is not his mother, he had just mixed them up and perceived her as such, and projected gestures, thoughts and attitudes onto his patient. There was no more space to perceive her as herself. Now he recalls that his patient had acted differently, e.g., when he had sent her to the laboratory. He will be more attentive to her individuality from now on. He has become curious. Most probably the next consultation will be a different encounter altogether without prejudice and with free floating attention.

This group work has revealed through setting the scene the transference and the counter-transference situation of the presenter. If we consider counter-transference, we assume that the patient has perceived the doctor as her son – her transference – and acts accordingly. The doctor would have reacted. On one hand this is a tool to interpret the patient's unconscious messages, on the other it is the self-experience part for the doctor to reflect on his own unconscious, which finally leads to a small, but considerable shift in the personality of the doctor (Balint 1957). The presenter has not been lectured, instead he was enabled to find out himself what had irritated him in the relationship and what had weighed him down. The observing group members were just as surprised.

There is no "clever group leader", who is able to detect the transference at once. He was merely attentive on a free floating level and ready to ask the question, which turned out to be relevant and meaningful. Insight could then be experienced and change of attitude was possible.

In France there is a society for "Balint work and Psychodrama", which is part of the International Balint Federation (IBF).

9.4 Imagination

It is proven that using the well-known technique of imagination is an interesting and effective tool for a Balint group, too. Once the presenter has finished his report of the patient, the group members are asked to close their eyes for five minutes and allow visual pictures of the story to arise. The pictures are then shared with the group and used for the discussion. The method encourages fantasies and perception of emotions and affect. Rational interpretations get more in the background, and a more emotional approach to the doctor–patient relationship is possible.

Example 21

A female gynecologist presents a 23-year-old woman who had come to the ward for delivery of her baby. There are no complications and the baby is healthy, but the mother turns away and cannot accept the child. The young doctor is appalled and does not understand. She feels angry towards the mother and worries for the child. The father does not show up, he is busy at work and does not take time to come to the hospital. The doctor feels helpless, wants to do something and eventually decides to refer mother and baby to a specialist clinic. She remains worried, helpless and angry. Asked about the parents of the patient, she replies that they had not been to the ward and she does not know anything about them.

In the imagination pictures emerge of Moses in a wicker basket. One group member sees two children in the hospital bed, another one reports to have imagined a desert. The pictures mainly show desolation, loneliness and emptiness. The following discussion reveals sadness. It becomes apparent that behind the prevailing anger towards the mother and worry about the child, lies deep sadness, which belongs to both the young mother and the presenting doctor. The doctor confirms that there is her own story in the background, which would explain her strong feelings, something she had not been aware of.

Imagination had led the group to more deep-seated emotions, which were not expressed in the report but could be sensed. The group touches the self-experience, the underlying story of the doctor, but does not discuss it. She understands by herself why her subconscious experiences had surfaced and that they would probably emerge again when working in obstetrics. After the group session she feels better prepared to deal with similar situations and will face reality.

Part III

Requirements for leading a Balint group

Chapter 10

Prerequisites

What attitude, knowledge and experience does a group leader need to bring to Balint group leading? Michael Balint had specialized in psychiatry, had undergone analytical training and had experience with general practitioners. At a later stage he extended his activities, learnt from working with colleagues in different countries and introduced his experiences and knowledge to others. Initially he had no doubt that group leaders had to be psychoanalysts. In his view, the group leader must be aware of the group process, he must understand what is happening in the relationship and must be able to recognize transference and counter-transference, including his own:

> Perhaps the most important factor is the behavior of the leader of the group. It is hardly an exaggeration to say that if he finds the right attitude he will teach more by his example than by everything else combined. After all, the technique we advocate is based on exactly the same sort of listening that we expect the doctors to learn and then to practice with their patients. By allowing everybody to be themselves, to have their say in their own way and in their own time, by watching for proper cues – that is, speaking only when something is really expected from him and making his point in a form which, instead of prescribing the right way, opens up possibilities for the doctors to discover by themselves some right way of dealing with the patient's problems – the leader can demonstrate in the "here and now" situation what he wants to teach.
>
> Obviously no one can live up to these exacting standards. Fortunately there is no need for perfection. The group leader may make mistakes – in fact he often does – without causing

much harm if he can accept criticism in the same or even somewhat sharper terms than he expects his group to accept.

(Balint 1957, p. 306)

Balint emphasizes that taking and giving time, patience and restraint
are the main characteristics of the leader. It is important that the
leader allows the group to work, gives enough time to each participant to express his thoughts and does not succumb to the temptation
to be too helpful, understanding or to support with too many of his
own ideas, and thus change the original group work into theoretical
lecturing, which would hinder the training process. There must be
space for emotions, free associations and fantasy. It is the leader's
responsibility to create this space by balancing the structuring of the
group process with giving the group the freedom they need to work
on the doctor–patient relationship at their own pace. This requires
sensitivity, intuition and experience from the leader. With his attitude, the leader creates an atmosphere in which each participant can
openly express what he thinks and feels, while his colleagues listen
with free floating attention, and at the same time concentrate on per-
ceiving their own subjective emotions.

Breaks and pauses in the flow of conversation are valuable; silence
has an important function and meaning. Tears get room and so do
aggression and happiness. The primary task of the doctors in the
group is not to understand the psychodynamics, but more so to
develop the "third ear", to "listen" to emotions and to the phenom-
ena of transference and counter-transference.

There is no doubt that the most important precondition for a
group leader's training is to have been a group member for a considerable time. Research has shown that the limited though considerable
change in the personality of the doctor – a shift in attitude – can only
be expected after at least one year of participation as a group member. Then the participant has internalized what he is experiencing in
the group: he listens differently, he perceives differently, he commu-
nicates with his patients and his colleagues in a different way. These
qualities are basic for starting the training and finally working as a
Balint group leader.

Chapter 11

Balint group leaders' training

In England, Balint groups were initially led by psychoanalysts. In the "second generation" general practitioners who had been students of Balint took over. Today it is seen as ideal in the United Kingdom that an analyst and a family doctor lead a group together in order to complement one another. In his essay "What Have the Romans Done for Us?", John Salinsky (2001) comments that the Balint Society in the UK has lost its analysts, however, and he wonders whether they have lost interest or whether the GPs have treated them badly saying: "We do not need you any longer, we are able to lead Balint groups on our own." Today the UK Balint Society is trying to encourage psychiatrists and psychoanalysts to join the ranks again as group members and to undergo group leaders' training.

Swiss Balint group leaders have to have completed psychotherapeutic or psychoanalytical training; then they work as co-leaders together with an experienced leader for a certain time before leadership workshops can be attended.

In Germany the requirements for joining the leaders' training are to be a medical specialist or a medical psychologist and to have had further education as a psychoanalyst or psychotherapist. Sufficient experience as a member of Balint groups is another important part.

France was one of the first countries to implement structured training, a curriculum, detailed qualification requirements and an admission committee. Two years of group membership is mandatory as well as analytical training. Non-doctors have to fulfill the same requirements, but are only allowed to lead groups for non-doctors.

Other countries have also started formalized education procedures. Sweden for example implemented their institutionalized two-year training schedule in 1998, which includes theoretical and practical teaching sessions.

In the USA, there are intensive training seminars twice yearly, at which international exchange and exposure is encouraged.

In 1997 the IBF (International Balint Federation) formulated guidelines for the accreditation of group leaders:

Guidelines for Accreditation of Balint Leaders (www.balintinternational.com):

1. Leaders should have appropriate basic training, e.g. Family Practitioner, Psychoanalyst, Psychotherapist, Psychologist.
2. Leaders should have prior experience of being in a Balint Group.
3. Leaders should have worked with an accredited leader for a sufficient period of time.
4. Leaders should have acquired an understanding of the Doctor–patient relationship.
5. Leaders should receive adequate supervision.

ALSO

Leaders should be able to demonstrate

a) that they create a safe and free environment within the group
b) that they focus the work on the Doctor–patient relationship rather than seek solutions
c) that they create a learning environment rather than resort to didactic teaching.

In 2009 at the International Balint Congress in Brasov, Romania, the IBF installed a working group (Andrew Elder, GB; Donald Nease, USA; Andre Matalon, Israel; Michel Delbrouck, Belgium; Heide Otten, Germany) with the mandate to further specify criteria for guidelines, international standards and an international curriculum for the training of Balint group leaders.

Since then, this group, together with the IBF, have promoted the exchange by organizing seminars every second year to intensify the discussion about techniques and training.

The German Balint Society stipulated the following criteria for accreditation (1 July 2011).

Requirements for doctors:

1. Membership in the German Balint Society.
2. Additional diploma in Psychotherapy and/or Psychoanalysis; or Specialist Doctor in Psychiatry and Psychotherapy or

Specialist Doctor in Child and Adolescent Psychiatry and Psychotherapy.
3. Three years of work experience after the qualifications mentioned in 2.
4. If, when obtaining the diploma in Psychoanalysis, Balint group work had not been required, documentation of 35 sessions of Balint group work with an accredited group leader (DBG) in a continuous working group.
5. Further 70 sessions of Balint group work in regular Balint groups, led by accredited leaders (DBG). These may be completed in weekend workshops.
6. Participation in six group leader seminars (DBG) with a minimum total of 30 sessions; documentation of having led two groups supervised by seminar leader.
7. Experience as co-leader at workshops or in continuous groups.
8. Accreditation will then be considered by the executive training committee of the DBG.

Requirements for qualified psychologists:

1. Medical Psychologist accredited for Analytical Psychotherapy by the Medical Council.
2. After qualification as per 1, three years of work experience in Analytical Psychotherapy.
3. Documentation of 105 sessions of Balint group work with a DBG accredited group leader.
4. 35 of the 105 sessions in a continuous Balint group.
5. Participation in six group leader seminars (DBG) with a minimum total of 30 sessions; documentation of having led two groups supervised by seminar leader.
6. Experience as co-leader at workshops or in continuous groups.
7. Accreditation will then be considered by the executive training committee of the DBG.

The criteria listed above are also recognized by the Medical Councils of the federal states in Germany. The accredited Balint group leader will have to supply his DBG accreditation certificate to the Medical Council. Then the participants in the groups he chairs will be able to use group participation for their postgraduate training. This is an important step, because Balint group work is an obligatory part of most postgraduate medical qualifications in Germany.

II.I Leaders' workshops

Leaders' workshops were developed by the German Balint Society in the 1970s supported by Swiss colleagues Arthur Trenkel and Hans Knoepfel, who had worked with Michael Balint in Sils Maria, Switzerland. The first German supervisors in the German leadership training were Peter Schneider, Bern Carrière and Werner Stucke. They built on Balint's idea of training doctors in a practical and "learning by doing" way.

At that time the leadership training groups consisted of twenty-four members, working – similar to the fishbowl groups – half in an inner and half in an outer circle. The inner circle would discuss a doctor–patient relationship under guidance of a leader and a co-leader, both in training. The members of the outer group observed the discussion, particularly with the focus on the leaders' behavior and actions: how did the attitude of the leaders influence the atmosphere in the group? How much was the group process influenced by the leaders' interventions? Was it possible for the working group to develop freely or did the leader try to bring them towards his own hypothesis or a solution? How did he manage to achieve the balance of structuring and letting things happen, between rigidity and chaos? Did he focus on the doctor–patient relationship? Did he protect the presenter? How did he deal with criticism towards himself?

All these questions were discussed with the big group straight after the group session, which in the case of leaders' workshops lasts 45–60 minutes. The discussion process was chaired by the experienced moderators whom I mentioned before.

The outer group now shared their observations according to the focus on leadership. The inner group responded with their own experience and perceptions: had they been able to associate freely, speak spontaneously and voice their "fresh thoughts" and fantasies? Or did they feel that the leader was insecure and they thus had to protect him?

The case presenter will also share how he experienced the group leaders during the discussion: did they look after him enough or did he feel attacked and unsafe? Or was he over protected: could he have been challenged more to get other new aspects?

Finally, leader and co-leader are asked how they experienced the group. How did they feel before starting the group? How did they perceive the case presentation? Did they develop a hypothesis regarding the difficult relationship which was presented? Did they try to push that hypothesis? Or was it possible for them to manage to stay open and to follow the process attentively? Were they relaxed enough to oscillate between their emotions and the meta-level? How was their relationship with the group members? And were the two of them well attuned or competing with each other? Did that have something to do with the case? And did that influence the group process?

This feedback is useful and important. The group leaders will receive a detailed commentary on how they were perceived, regardless of how much or how little they have been saying. Balint on this point advised the leaders "to merge into the group". They are always present as leading figures anyway.

If the leaders are insecure the group will either become chaotic or some group members will become saviors, possibly competing with each other. This dynamic then does not mirror the case but is attributed to the attitude of the group leaders.

John Salinsky told a joke about two viola players to demonstrate what it can mean, when a leader "merges into the group" (Balint 1957):

> Once upon a time, there was a viola player, who wished nothing more than to conduct the orchestra – which he had been a part of for many years – for just one day. His wish came true, when the conductor fell ill and he took his chance. For four weeks he stood on the podium and was very happy. Then the conductor returned and satisfied the viola player went back to his place. The other viola player from the desk next to him turned to face him and asked him with astonishment: "Hey, where have you been all this time?"
>
> (Salinsky, personal message)

Is that the ideal Balint group leader, who is not perceived as a conductor? Apparently the orchestra had played well. At the very least, the conductor had not been disturbing. He had not absorbed attention, but given space for the members' qualities to shine. A good Balint group leader values the statements of each member, accompanies the process verbally and non-verbally, gives structure and a frame and brings the discussion back to the doctor–patient relationship whenever necessary. When the leader stays passive only, the process may be lively but too chaotic, resulting in uncertainty and frustration.

When the leader is too much the focus, group interaction might be stifled as the group members only connect with the leader. Then there is no analytic group process, dynamics fail and the mirroring of the doctor–patient relationship in the group does not happen and is not available.

The report of the presenter paints an emotional picture for the group, which each member perceives in a different way. In the group discussion each member represents one color of the picture, and thus mirrors the system, which has been presented, with all its conscious and unconscious emotions, and develops it in front of the presenter's eyes. To achieve insightful mirroring, a safe and creative space needs to be secured by the leader.

For the leader, it is fundamental to acknowledge that the experts are sitting in the group. Balint emphasized that he as group leader learned a lot from the family doctors – and I need to add from today's perspective: from all specialists attending Balint groups. If the leader presents himself as a psychoanalytical expert, important aspects from the practical work and the described dynamics get lost and the process becomes a lecture.

To make use of the group process as a mirror for the doctor–patient relationship, to encourage fantasies, associations and the emotions of the participants for this purpose is the task of the group leader. At the same time he has the duty to protect the presenter to enable him to concentrate on his own emotional reactions to the group work and possibly understand through the "parallel process" how the patient feels and what is his situation.

For this purpose the presenter is invited to "push back" once the case has been presented and questions have been answered. The group members are asked not to address the presenter and not to involve him directly in the discussion.

This enables the group to unfold their fantasies, and the presenter to fully concentrate on his own emotional reactions. He then does not have to defend, justify or explain more details. He will not be forgotten in his position, but always watched carefully in his reactions by the leader and co-leader. They might address him saying: "Well, just listen to what your colleague feels; that is her perception and must not be true for you." Or: "At the moment it might be very difficult for you to remain silent; please let me know when it becomes unbearable." The presenter feels understood and protected and the group can continue "thinking fresh"; the atmosphere stays benevolent.

The pushback is flexible; the presenter can always be brought back into the discussion. It needs a sensitive leader to decide when and how it is beneficial for the group process. A strict rule to only ask the presenter back for a final statement would narrow the process and limit the chances for feedback and additional interesting information.

Balint in his groups had often asked the presenter to listen silently to the group discussion.

The well-trained and experienced leader oscillates during the group process between emotion and reason, observation and analysis, between reality and meta-level. The well-trained leader, who finally leads groups on his own, has to be aware of all the influences on his group work, which he had learned by the feedback given in leaders' seminars from the supervisors, the group members, the presenter and his co-leader. He must recognize what effects his interventions have. He can say and do whatever he wishes as long as he is aware of the consequences, and stays responsible for the group and the presenter. His attentiveness and thoughtfulness together with a relaxed attitude give him the opportunity to have everything in sight, to let it go and still influence the process. With so much to do, having a co-leader is very helpful, as long as they have a good cooperation.

"Fortunately there is no need for perfection. The group leader may make mistakes – in fact he often does – without causing much harm" as Balint stated. Especially in the leaders' seminars the participants profit from mistakes – or maybe it is better to say the failure or imperfection – the most; they are important and helpful whenever the critics from the group and from the supervisors are accepted as a precious contribution.

The main task of the group is to work for the presenter. A failure of the group leader could be to lose sight of the doctor–patient relationship, by discussing cultural or health-political issues or by allowing the introduction of a second case, which distracts from the original story.

The protection of the presenter must be guaranteed. If this is not the case, the group or the presenter will voice their criticism: "After this experience, I am much more reluctant to present a case." Of course the group members also need protection to feel free for associations. If the leaders harshly reject fantasies or judge upon comments the group work will suffer. Negative emotions like anger and aggression can possibly be reconnected to the case and to the mirroring of the relationship. Differences of opinion and arguments can thus be used to understand the case and the relationship, and maybe used in a role-play. Mutual esteem and respect are the essential conditions for the success of Balint group work.

Part of group leader training is to have experienced all positions in the process: group member, presenter, leader, co-leader and supervisor. Attending six leaders' workshops with thirty sessions guarantee that all trainees will have had that opportunity.

Originally groups at trainer workshops consisted of twenty-four members. Today we keep numbers down to twelve to fifteen. We find the atmosphere with this number more trusting and the training more constructive. Two to three participants sit outside and observe the process.

Everyone has the chance to be heard in the feedback discussion, and there is less competition than in the larger groups. Constructive critique in smaller groups is far more easily accepted.

Joachim Bauer (2004) researched the teacher–pupil relationship and found results which also apply to our leaders' workshops: if stress systems are activated, learning becomes more difficult and achievements are lessened. A warm and friendly environment in the workshops encourages constructive critique and humor. This leads to positive motivation and successful learning. And that is the same for Balint groups in general.

The co-leaders' position is not clearly defined. Leader and co-leader will ideally fine-tune their cooperation and they may share or divide their tasks. The co-leader might be asked to keep track of the time frame and the doctor–patient relationship, watch the presenter, while he is in the push-back position or encourage group members who are not contributing. Like the leader, he will be asked to hold back his own hypothesis or solutions.

When working in continuous groups the leader will be able to choose whom he wants to work with: someone he likes or has cooperated with before. They will exchange and discuss their perceptions of the group process afterwards.

At leaders' workshops, the situation is different, as leaders have to co-work with others, whom they might have never even met before. This constellation can highlight important aspects and conflicts. Often we see competition between the leaders: who guides the group with his interventions? Whose hypothesis are they following? Did I understand the other co-leader's hypothesis? Have I been able to perceive it? Does the one leader see his co-leader as too passive and believe that more structure is needed? How will he deal with it? Maybe the co-leader will become more active and impose his structure on the process. How is the leader going to deal with it? Is the group aware of the conflict? And does it affect their work? With an open and sympathetic cooperation between the two leaders the group feels more secure and freedom of thought and expression increase.

Leader and co-leader sit opposite to each other in the circle, both have a good view of at least half of the group and their angles and perspectives should complement each other. Their communication is verbal and non-verbal. The group benefits from good contact. If, for example, the co-leader notices that the leader is emotionally too absorbed by the process he may temporarily take the lead. This sensitivity and good cooperation may serve as an example for teamwork in everyday life.

Whenever a conflict between the leaders appears, this may be a reflection of the presented doctor–patient relationship and thus should be verbalized to clarify the situation. It could also be a conflict arising from the personality of the leaders and would then distract from the case. Observations like this will be exposed and discussed in the leadership training and are important for practical co-leadership.

To train for leadership it is helpful to work as co-leader together with an experienced leader in an ongoing group for some time. The observation of such a group working and the exchange with the group leader afterwards is a different experience from co-leading in a workshop.

Leaders' workshops consist of doctors and psychologists with long-standing experience as Balint group members, wanting to further their skills and become leaders themselves. Training in this context is valuable but is different from "real life". Continuous groups consist of members with varying backgrounds, many participants are new to the field and not every member is really there of his own free accord. A lot can be learnt in these groups by taking up co-leadership with an experienced leader. Motivation of group members can take center stage in beginner groups, particularly when obligatory attendees are present. New members may be skeptical and not really sure what to expect and what is expected of them.

Also the cases in ongoing groups are different to the ones presented at leaders' workshops, at which psychiatric or psychotherapeutic relationships are mostly discussed and where the group members are familiar with the structure of the group work.

In ongoing groups we get in- or out-patients from many different specialties. The cases may be offered not with a difficulty in the relationship but as "difficult patients" or a "sad and unsolvable case" or "a mistake". A question may arise: "What can I do?" – and that again is a temptation for the group leader to lecture or for the group to give good advice. It is not always easy then to remember and stick to the task of analyzing the doctor–patient relationship.

Leaders' workshops are open for the participation of experienced leaders, too. Working on their own may lead them to realize that they need to be monitored and supervised in the leader's or co-leader's position, getting feedback and exchanging views with colleagues.

11.2 Supervision for Balint group leaders

Another possibility for group leaders to get feedback on their group work is offered in supervision groups. Those provide the opportunity to discuss difficulties in the groups at home and with single group members. The structure and proceedings are similar to that of a usual Balint group. One member of the supervision group presents his Balint group or one of the members in his group as the case, and then the colleagues work on the relationship with associations, fantasies and pictures in the usual way.

Example 22

A group leader talks about a group member who never brings his own emotions or fantasies, but rather comments on and interprets other members' input. This causes a lot of confusion and the leader feels quite angry about it at times. She wonders how she might be able to engage the colleague in a more constructive manner. She mentions that he is head of a department in an institution and has presented a few patients but also shared his thoughts about a colleague. He has managed to receive a special status in the group. In the supervision group the impression is expressed that he might need this special status to overcome insecurity and the fear of becoming embarrassed and humiliated. In the group, he prefers to take the position of a co-leader and thus competes with the leader in order to protect himself. With these new perspectives the anger of the presenter diminishes. Maybe the group member will eventually be able to relinquish his present position and become more open and constructive. Maybe it just needs more time. She does not have to compete with him as long as she is content and happy with her position as the group leader. You are lonely at the top. And she has to admit that sometimes she would rather be a group member, fantasize and think afresh, instead of keeping up the exhausting position of analytic abstinence and responsibility. The difficult group member might prefer to hide behind the analytic position.

Relationships between a group leader and his group as well as between a group leader and the group members are characterized by sometimes difficult interactions, by unconscious emotions, by transference and counter-transference.

Supervision groups can help to shift those emotions into consciousness. Constructive group work will subsequently be much easier again and helpful for the group leader, who is the presenter in the supervision group, as well as for his Balint group and, last but not least, for the doctor–patient relationships discussed in his groups.

Part IV

Results and opportunities

Chapter 12

Research findings

Research is the planned search for new insights.

Is it really a new discovery that the doctor as a person has an effect on the patient? Has that not always been implicit knowledge? What was new about Balint's request to study the psychological problems in general practice compared with what has been perceived until then?

Balint started as a natural scientist and transferred the approach and methods he learnt in biochemical research to his investigation with the group of general practitioners. He was not searching for a philosophical or literary description of the phenomenon, but for scientific proof of the efficacy of the doctor as a drug, with effects and side effects.

He set three tasks for the training cum research groups:

1. to examine the psychological problems in general practice
2. to train general practitioners for this research
3. to develop appropriate training and research methods

Initially, the group in London discussed the drugs usually prescribed by practitioners.

> The discussion quickly revealed – certainly not for the first time in the history of medicine – that by far the most frequently used drug in general practice was the doctor himself, i.e. that it was not only the bottle of medicine or the box of pills that mattered, but the way the doctor gave them to his patient – in fact, the whole atmosphere in which the drug was given and taken. ...
>
> The seminar, however, soon went on to discover that no pharmacology of this important drug exists yet. ... no

guidance whatever is contained in any text-book as to the dosage in which the doctor should prescribe himself, in what form, how frequently, what his curative and his maintenance doses should be, and so on. Still more disquieting is the lack of any literature on the possible hazards of this kind of medication, on the various allergic conditions met in individual patients which ought to be watched carefully, or on the undesirable side-effects of the drug.

(Balint 1957, p. 1)

In Berlin, Michael Balint had worked in biochemical and pharmacological research with Otto Warburg. He had studied the effects and side effects of drugs. He pointed out the interaction of medication and doctor, pharmacology and psychology, natural science and psychoanalysis. This had become his research focus: here he was looking for answers. Not one or the other but the interplay of both. Together with his "training cum research group" he wanted to design the pharmacology of the drug "doctor": "Thus, the research could be conducted only by general practitioners while doing their everyday work, undisturbed and unhampered, sovereign masters of their own surgeries" (Balint 1957, p. 3).

Soon it became clear that, quite unlike in pharmacology, the "drug" doctor could not be standardized. Rather, the effects and side effects were very individual. Every doctor has to gather his own experiences, and has a chance to look at them with "new eyes". Balint and his group managed to elevate the doctor–patient relationship to its rightful place in diagnosis and therapy and to encourage further research.

Ulrich Rosin elaborated on this concept (Rosin 1989). Primarily, he summarized the few existing scientific research results on this subject. He describes an increase in empathic competence in Balint group members as the only tangible finding. His initial aim had been to observe group members' and leaders' attitudes directly during the sessions, to tape the sessions and reconstruct implicit subjective theories and styles of the leaders. This proved practically impossible. He therefore confined himself to developing a self-rating questionnaire for group members and group leaders. The simple outcome was what others had described before: "Balint groups are good."

A question not answered remained: "What is the effectiveness of the Balint group method and does it have an impact on medical care – diagnostic and therapy – in general?"

In 1979, Balint work was incorporated into the curriculum for the diploma of psychotherapeutic care in Germany. In 1987 the "psychosomatic basic training" became part of the postgraduate training of all doctors working together with the health insurances, and Balint group work is an important part of this training. In 1993 *R. Obliers et al.* started to research "the development of the medical conversation in general practice by Balint group participation" (Obliers et al. 1996). They compared video-documented first general practice consultations before and after one year of weekly Balint group membership, to investigate changes in communication characteristics.

Their hypothesis was: by working in Balint groups the doctor increases his capability to consciously perceive his personal experience in the contact and his affective resonance towards patient behavior, to reflect on his relationship with the patient and to change towards a more patient-centered view and consultation style, through stronger orientation towards the patient as a person with an illness.

They investigated doctor–patient discourses regarding linguistic and communicational differences between first interviews before and one year after Balint group work. They focused on the quality and the course of the postulated processes of change.

The extensive study revealed the following results: after one year of Balint work the percentage of doctor talk in the first meeting with the patient was reduced from 43% to 27%, thus increasing the word space for the patient from 57% to 73%. The patient had more say and the doctor listened more. Doctors gave the patient more time and space to develop their own contributions to the consultation and disturbed or inhibited them far less with questions, when describing their symptoms and complaints.

Also the substantive conversation categories were evaluated, and it turns out that, after one year of Balint group participation, the doctors used fewer leading questions and increasingly followed the patient's information and perspective, rather than sticking to their own thought sequences and apostolic function. They focused more on the experience and perception of the patient. The doctor's interest in the somatic aspects of illness did not take a back seat but his questions regarding the patient's views and living conditions increased. The spectrum was expanded by taking the psychological and social components into account without using more time for the consultation.

The cooperation with the patient became more effective.

This research shows that doctors changed their communication attitudes and behavior towards their patients through Balint work, which was shown by subjective rating and objective observation methods. This seems to confirm Balint's thesis of a "considerable, though limited change of personality".

Dorte Kjeldmand researched the effect of Balint groups in southern Sweden from 1997 to 2006 (Kjeldmand 2006), where she has worked as a general practitioner since 1981.

She investigated two groups of general practitioners, one with and the other without Balint group participation, by using a questionnaire regarding the following topics:

- work pressure
- control, self-determination, heteronomy
- satisfaction
- quality
- cooperation and support
- further education, training
- work and health

Another questionnaire was answered by group members and leaders and related to the following:

- What happens in the groups and how?
- Is the effect measurable?
- What happens when doctors meet in a Balint group?
- What happens to the personality of the doctor?
- Are holistic doctors "born" in Balint groups?

Research 1:
Twenty Balint group members were compared to twenty-one general practitioners without Balint group experience with a self-rating questionnaire. The result showed that Balint doctors were happier in their work and felt more in control of their work situation. They valued their own capacity to treat psychosomatic patients more highly in comparison with the control group. The differences increased the longer the group participation lasted.

Research 2:
The second investigation centered on the question: "How patient-centered am I?", and resulted in a tool for training programs, to

appraise the development of young doctors and to detect early signs of burn-out.

Research 3:
This consisted of nine interviews with general medical practitioners, the scripts of which were analyzed. The doctors described their Balint training as helpful and essential for their work life, in terms of competence, professional identity and a sense of certainty, enabling them to experience and retain joy in their work.

Research 4:
Fifty-one Balint group leaders answered a questionnaire and eight were interviewed regarding their difficulties in leading the group with regard to members dropping out of groups. Individual reasons for leaving the group were given. Some left the group because they were dissatisfied with the method: they longed for more teaching. Others left because there were difficulties in the group dynamics, which they could not work through. There were significant differences between groups of voluntary members and those where membership was obligatory for further specialist training.

Dorte Kjeldmand's study looked at self-evaluation of doctors regarding their feeling competent, their self-regulation and prevention of burn-out through support and exchange with colleagues. Most group members appraised the group work positively in this respect. But not all doctors benefited from group membership. There was a risk that stressful group situations had hurt them and this was why they had left.

An important conclusion: Balint group leaders need to be aware of this and they should have ongoing training and supervision.

This research was not aligned to the question of whether there is a benefit to the patients when their doctor participates in a Balint group. Meaningful investigations are lacking in this respect. A conclusion may be possible from the findings, that doctors felt better, more competent and experienced more satisfaction from their interactions with patients. One might expect that the quality of diagnosis and treatment might also improve. However, further research to test this hypothesis would be necessary but not easy.

In Germany a study was started in 2004 by the German Balint Society (DBG) sending questionnaires to 503 accredited Balint group leaders. It gives an impression of practical Balint group work

all over Germany and in the weekend workshops offered by the DBG. A total of 333 questionnaires were sent back, which is a feedback of 66.2% (Häfner et al. 2009).
Questions for example were:

- Who leads Balint groups today?
- What characteristics do leaders have, what describes them socio-demographically?
- How do leaders shape the session? Do they add creative elements like role-play, sculpturing or imagination?

In total, 30.6% of the leaders were specialists in psychosomatic medicine and psychotherapy, 17.1% were specialists in psychiatry and psychotherapy, 12.3% were general practitioners, a few were ophthalmologists or urologists, none were surgeons, 5.4% were psychological psychotherapists.

Each Balint group leader had 1.34 groups on average (0–9).

Fifty-nine percent of the leaders were male and 41% were female. The average age was 57.2 (39–90); 58 (17.4%) were more than 65 years old.

The average number of registered members per group was 10.7, whereas the average number of active members in the group was 8.6.

Eighty-five percent of group sessions last 90 minutes, 4.4% last 180 minutes, 3.3% 120 minutes, 1.8% 45 minutes and 1.5% 60 minutes.

One question related to whether additional methods taken from psychotherapy were integrated into the sessions.

Role-play (15.3%), imagination (13.8%), sculpture (6.6%) and psychodrama (4.5%) were the most frequently added methods; less frequently mentioned were focusing, family therapy, group analysis, body therapy, painting, music, systemic elements, techniques from behavioral therapy, problem solving strategies, talk therapy, reflecting team and supervision.

This shows the possibility of different individual approaches to Balint group work.

The most common frequency of meetings was one session every fortnight. Psychoanalysts as Balint group leaders are not very common any more. Most groups were heterogeneous, which shows that Balint work today is interesting for all medical specialists and non-medical professionals, not only for general practitioners and psychotherapists (Häfner et al. 2009).

Donald Nease from the USA reported at the International Balint Congress in Stockholm in 2005 a study on "Researching the 'Pharmacology' of Balint work in the United States" (Nease 2005).

Within the USA, Balint groups are very common in postgraduate training, most prevalently in family medicine, but increasingly also in gynecology and obstetrics and in pediatrics training. Initially, Balint group leadership was researched in terms of defining the essential elements of effective group leadership. Criteria for leaders' training and credentialing standards were developed following the results. Data were obtained from mutual observation by experienced leaders. Topics were highlighted which are common to other small groups: confidentiality, safety, responsibility for establishing and maintaining group norms, etc. Differences in Balint group leadership were also established: a focus on understanding rather than problem solving, avoidance of leader initiated psychological probing of individual group members, and keeping the group responsible for the work of the presenter's case. This research on the characteristics of effective Balint group leadership has begun to establish the "active ingredients" of a well-run Balint group. In pharmacological terms, an understanding of the active ingredients allows one to begin to study the effects of these active ingredients.

The question for further research would be: "Does Balint group participation result in changes in empathy, openness to psychological issues, and the ability to tolerate uncertainty?"

First of all a degree of change has to be established. "What is the effect size of Balint group membership on any of these individual domains?"

Standardized questionnaires were completed by Family Medicine residents participating in Balint groups over a two-year period. The results were presented at the International Congress in Brasov in 2009: although the small number of respondents made usual statistical comparisons not possible, a clear trend could be shown "for a modest improvement in the cohorts' empathy and psychological mindedness over the two year period" (Nease et al. 2009).

Further research is necessary and has been planned.

Vladimir Vinokur from St Petersburg in Russia, presented his qualitative study at the International Congress in Berlin in 2003: "Evaluation of the Effectiveness of Balint Groups in Different Social Professionals" (Vinokur 2003, pp. 147–151).

The groups consisted of different kinds of professionals: general physicians, consultants, psychiatrists and psychotherapists, medical psychologists and teachers, in total eight groups.

The study aimed to seek answers to the following questions:

- Are there any differences between social professionals in sensitivity to Balint work?
- How do Balint groups exert their effect?
- What does their effectiveness consist of?
- How could we test the effectiveness of instruments used to measure the effectiveness of Balint groups?

The groups consisted of eight to fourteen members; they met for up to three years twice a month for three hours each time. The participants were informed about the psychoanalytical and group-analytical background of Balint work, mainly regarding psychological defenses and resistances and the unconscious sources of their communication issues.

The research tool was a semi-structured interview and a specially designed questionnaire containing twenty-nine items, investigating different aspects of professionals' feelings and thoughts related to their job. They further used a Coping styles inventory and a Conflict management styles inventory.

Results showed positive changes after the course of Balint work in all groups, with interesting differences between the professions. All groups showed improvement in communication skills, and an increase in self-esteem, self-awareness, job satisfaction and job effectiveness. In some cases an increase in cost-effectiveness was reported. Less pressure of psychological and interpersonal conflicts was also found. These positive changes were highly significant in the groups of general physicians and teachers. Interestingly, the improvement was larger, the more problematic the situation of general practitioners and teachers had been at the start of the study:

> The prevalence of different coping styles in all groups of professionals after a course of Balint work tends to balance, that means the appearance of more harmony in people's emotional reactions, conceptions and thoughts and behavior when they are facing communicative problems or puzzles. (Vinokur 2003, p. 150)

In terms of conflict management all groups started out from the relatively high prevalence of unfavorable styles like competition and yielding. General practitioners and teachers had the least tendency to achieve compromise- and cooperation-strategies. After Balint group membership all groups showed beneficial tendencies to improve conflict management strategies.

"The outcomes of the research are helpful for the promotion of Balint work in different regions of Russia" and Balint work has been incorporated into undergraduate and postgraduate training programs since then (Vinokur 2003, p. 151).

John Salinsky from London reported in Stockholm 2005 about "the new and exciting research, that the group in London had been engaged on in the last three years". They decided to appoint an experienced qualitative researcher, Ruth Pinder, to carry out the project. She was an ethnographer and watched the "Balint tribe" – a Balint group at work.

Now, what did she observe?

> She noted that the doctors were given the opportunity to talk about patients who were bothering them; they were allowed to talk about their feelings; they were encouraged to take their time; their stories were received sympathetically and non-judgmentally. They were supported by a group to which they felt they belonged. They were encouraged to see their patients as people who had a life and relationships outside the surgery. The discussion about the patients' lives and their interaction with the doctor had a richness and a complexity not normally found in medical presentations. In the group, they were invited to express their feelings and also to imagine how the patient was feeling. The doctors were also relieved to find that other group members were struggling with the same problems. It was also useful to be able to hear so many different ideas and points of view. It made them think.

Another very interesting remark of the supervising ethnographer was that the stories she heard from the presenters in the group told more than an "individual's unique experience, they are also telling us about the society they come from, the time and the place and the values of the people concerned".

And her conclusion for qualitative research on a Balint group at work was that:

> this kind of learning is a gradual process in which the Balint influence mingles and interacts with learning from other sources.
>   This means that the results can't properly be captured by methods that try to identify short-term changes in doctors' attitudes or behavior.
>
> (Salinsky et al. 2005, pp. 77–88)

Benyamin Maoz from Israel, at the 15th International Balint Congress in Lisbon in 2007, remembered his colleague Tomi Spencer, who in his last years had struggled for a scientific evaluation of Balint groups. His main trend had been qualitative research in Family Medicine. He met resistance in the Israeli Balint community. And Benyamin followed the question why this deep, not entirely conscious resistance to any research plan was there. On the one hand they felt:

> in Israel more and more the pressure and demand to prove to the health services and to the medical and academic establishment the validity of Balint groups, so that it is really worthwhile to spend money and time for the training and continual activity of these.

On the other hand unresolved problems were:

> How can we measure the outcome of Balint groups? If we maintain that the members of a Balint group will become "better doctors", how can we measure that? Measuring the satisfaction of their patients? Is it a measure of a "better doctor"? Measuring the doctors' feelings of professional satisfaction, etc.? Measuring the doctors' feelings of burn-out? Is there a scale to measure it?

Spencer had encouraged group members to anonymously write down one sentence after each session they had attended, to answer the question: "What are you taking home from this group session?" (Maoz et al. 2007, pp. 29–32).

We have taken this on board and included the question in the German Balint Group's evaluation form for Balint workshops since 2008. To illustrate the importance of reflective psychodynamic group work, some comments are listed below, many from Balint "novices":

"What are you taking home from this group work?"

- inspiration, support, new ideas for day to day work in the hospital
- more focus on the relationship and on own shares in it, empathy for the patient
- enables new perspectives beyond the own imagination, new ways of looking at things, courage to stand by your own impressions and thoughts, relief
- plenty of material to think about, impulses for the professional development
- that you are not alone with your problems
- concepts against speechlessness, relief from your own helplessness in the doctor–patient relationship
- confirmation for my career aspiration, plenty of vitality, the feeling that the weekend was worthwhile, the process is moving on
- to give emotions more space in the daily work, to look for a continuous group close to home
- getting away from egocentrism, impulses to respect and value different points of view, increase in certainty, changed self-reflection
- not necessarily ready made solution; still have lots of unprocessed feelings but they are clearer and have a name now, which is absolutely necessary for digesting them. The group was open and had a positive attitude and good coherence, not least through the highly professional but warm hearted leadership
- many suggestions and challenges, desire for more work, good mood, lively and relevant experiences, valuable and appreciative feedback
- a sense of competence, and at the same time being allowed to make mistakes
- gives practical impulses for everyday work, good possibilities to disentangle complicated situations
- that the leader is important for the group's success
- insight into problems I am not confronted with daily, better understanding of psychosomatic illnesses, better self-evaluation
- chance of more humorous dealing with matters, more pleasure at work again
- a new window has been opened, more interest awakened, want more depth and to value my work more positively, more understanding for difficult cases
- helpful experiences, but also the experience that doctors do not keep together, that there are prejudices; encouragement for more constructive topical discourse
- support and back-up, being understood

- the doctor's psychological health was so far no significant factor, but it is vital – the doctor is a human being, too, and not a machine
- desire for more Balint work, the diversity in the group was helpful, new ways, refreshed curiosity in the doctor–patient relationship
- high degree of self-experience, not always having to fulfill all expectations of patients
- interesting insight into psychotherapeutic care of cancer patients, that gives hope
- so much inspiration, to take more time and be more mindful, for my patients and for myself, attention – outside; mindfulness inside
- increased understanding for group work, taking controversial view-points on board, even without presenting a case I gained important insights and relations to me as a person
- courage to look at relationships with purpose, despite my defenses
- I found that I could empathize with patients, which I had never previously experienced. The many ideas and aspects of the group members paint a multi-layered picture of the patient and the doctor. I felt well received by the group and the leader
- it is very helpful, when professionals from different backgrounds are in a group
- again the experience, that Balint group work offers practical help for my daily work

Guido Flatten from Germany started to collect data in 2012 to evaluate the impact of Balint sessions on the group members. A total of 107 accredited Balint group leaders, namely doctors, handed out recently developed questionnaires for Balint group sessions survey. They collected the feedback of 1,443 participants in 384 different Balint groups. The questionnaire includes four relevant dimensions of Balint group work: 1. change in own perception, 2. reflection of the dynamics of the doctor–patient relationship, 3. mirroring of the presented case in the group dynamics, 4. self-perception of own professional role.

In total, 72.4% of the group members were somatic doctors, 21.3% were psychiatrists, psychosomatic physicians and psychotherapists. Most of the participants were general practitioners (33.2%).

Results so far: somatic doctors demonstrated more significant records with regard to consciousness of change in own perception, reflection of the dynamic of the doctor–patient relationship and self-perception of own professional role as compared to psychosomatic physicians and psychotherapists. All doctors who presented a case are related to significantly high scores in all four dimensions.

Eighty percent of all participants showed highest scores (4 and 5 scores on a 5-point scale) on the question: Do you like participating in Balint groups?

The impact mentioned above is irrespective of whether the participation was mandatory or voluntary.

This feedback from Balint group members and the above mentioned research is encouraging to continue Balint group work, and to support a profound Balint leadership training. The leaders carry great responsibility; particularly in respect of our aim to make Balint work an important part of postgraduate training in all social professions (Flatten et al. 2015).

Chapter 13

Balint group work with other professionals

Do professional relationships in social jobs have something in common? Are there particular problems in relationships in those social occupations? There is a joint purpose from both sides – doctor and patient, teacher and parent, solicitor and client, pastor and member of congregation. The illness needs to be conquered, the student prepared for life's reality, the court case won and the spiritual crises overcome. Problems emerge when unconscious processes endanger this common goal. At the start of vocational training in the helping professions, an idealistic view often prevails: to lead children into a better future, to eliminate the injustice in the world and to further faith in the good.

Investigations on medical students have shown that initial idealism often turns into cynicism during their studies. Increasing self-experience, work experience and pragmatic realism finally and hopefully lead to the attitude: "I am doing this as well as possible." Balint himself spoke of the "good enough doctor".

Balint work encourages the realistic view and self-reflection which leads to "the limited, though considerable change of personality".

Research done by Joachim Bauer in Freiburg (2004) demonstrated that teachers have a high willingness to overextend themselves and therefore show a high risk of burn-out.

The study differentiates four types of teachers:

* *Type G* shows high engagement in the job and willingness to commit himself to the process; s/he is able though to keep sufficient distance and therefore recovers during leisure time. S/he values cooperation with colleagues and experiences success at work.
* *Type A* often has perfectionist attitudes as well as willingness to overexert himself at work above average, and has lost his ability

to recover. S/he tends to act as "lone fighter", experiences little support and is threatened by wear.

- *Type B* has worked despite continued overexertion and developed psychophysical fatigue. Coupled with resignation he has lost the ability to work effectively and cannot profit from his colleagues' support.
- *Type S* fears occupational wear and tear. Those colleagues usually do their job correctly, but they do not show the tendency to overextend themselves.

Teachers benefit from Balint groups, supervision and coaching, because their central problem is to shape the relationship with pupils and with parents, besides the cooperation with colleagues and the structural framework.

It became clear, that teachers – not least because of a lot of administrative pressure – tend to neglect reflecting on and consciously shaping relationships with pupils and parents, and concentrate instead on imparting knowledge. This attitude has a negative influence on the learning atmosphere.

Many teachers are uncertain whether and how to introduce their personality and authenticity into their teaching. Parents often are not supportive, but rather distrustful and controlling. Consequently teachers retreat into a position of "invulnerable lack of identity". This cannot be productive in terms of effective teaching.

(Bauer 2004)

For some years there was a model of "prophylactic health measures for teachers" in Freiburg, which included lectures, seminars and Balint groups. It became apparent that teachers are often enmeshed in a web of complicated relationships: in the first place with pupils, then with parents, colleagues, the headmaster, the school counselor, the Ministry of Education and other politicians.

Joachim Bauer, who initiated the above mentioned project, is a neuroscientist. He infers that shaping relevant relationships is responsible for the activation of positive or negative motivational systems in our body with according consequences. Recognition and compassion increase motivation. Rejection and hostility activate the stress system, learning and teaching are thus made more difficult and results suffer. This process influences teachers as well as students.

According to pediatricians from Stuttgart, who made an investigation – supported by the Stuttgart Health Board – 51% of 2,000 children suffered from psychosomatic health issues ("Jugendgesundheitsstudie Stuttgart" – youth health study (www.stuttgart.de)).

The aim of the Freiburg model of "prophylactic health measures for teachers" was to improve the learning environment for pupils and teachers.

Example 23

A female teacher shares that she experiences difficulties particularly with adolescent girls during puberty. She is annoyed by the lack of seriousness and does not sympathize at all with their whispering and giggling. In particular, the 15-year-old Tanja from grade 8 is bothersome for her. Tanja is a single child, spoiled by her parents and apparently never criticized at home. At school she puts in very little effort but is intelligent enough always to just make the grade. She provokes the teacher and leaves no doubt that she does not take any advice from her. The teacher has lost composure more than once and fears that she will lose control; one time she had yelled at the girl. She promptly complained to her parents, they called the headmaster, and the headmaster had invited the teacher to talk. He had been understanding but made it clear that this happening was unique, and her loss of control would not be accepted, if repeated. Her anger towards the student had grown, she would prefer not to see her again, but had to "suffer" her until the end of the school year.

The Balint group consisted of five female and three male teachers from different schools. At first, they looked at the reaction of the headmaster. One female teacher reported similar difficulties and suggested a meeting together with the parents. The pupil would not benefit from further protection. "Well, that's the way it goes today", comments another female colleague, "good education is no longer important, the school has to please the parents these days. To constructively criticize pupils is no longer accepted." In her day that had been different, her parents had been called into school when she had been flippant towards teachers at that age, and she received a good hard reprimand back at home. Others agree. A male teacher mentions girls who had tried to provoke him with obscene gestures and sexual remarks. Sometimes he could take that on the chin with humor, but at other times he simply did not feel like it. He feared that his reactions could be misinterpreted and he might get into difficulties with parents and with the school management. A discussion ensued in the group about how things have changed for the worse; lack of discipline, vulnerability and difficult learning environments are mentioned. The stress the presenter has to endure, when she swallows her anger, becomes a theme in the group.

The presenting teacher had listened with interest, and she recalled events from her own time at school. She was contemplative. Would she really welcome the old times back? Maybe she envies the girl. Would she not have liked more freedom for herself and today's possibilities and ease, and parents who always supported her? She begins to see the pupil in a fresh light. When asked whether she would like to swap with her, she says "no". She can think of aspects in which her student's life is more difficult, more complex and more exhausting compared to how her own had been. Her student might well be more anxious and fearful than she had been. She realizes that she had been constantly comparing herself with the girl, and just acknowledged her in this competition. Does she really know her? Prejudiced, she had certainly cast her in the role of a spoiled pubescent single child; now she had become interested in the real person.

Transference, counter-transference and identification. The group realized the underlying pattern of the relationship. It becomes clear that unconscious feelings, like envy, play an important role in how the relationship is shaped. It is not easy and needs a trusting and non-judgmental environment to bring those feelings to light. The staff-room is certainly not that holding, supportive setting. Often relationships with colleagues are too complicated and dominate the interactions. Team supervision and coaching for staff would be useful. Balint groups need the opportunity to free associate and to "think fresh". Mixed groups consisting of teachers from different schools or other professions offer a promising alternative.

As mentioned before, the research from Vladimir Vinokur in St Petersburg showed that teachers are the ones who profit from Balint group work the most – besides general practitioners. They gain self-esteem, self-awareness, conflict resolution strategies and attentiveness for psychological problems (Vinokur 2003).

An article published in the *Balint Journal* in 2009 reported on a group of ten family lawyers, who asked Dankwart Mattke, an experienced Balint group leader in Munich, to chair their group

(Mattke et al. 2009). They wanted to look at their problems with their clients. They complained that their legal education had not covered any psychological aspects, although in their daily work all lawyers and judges were expected to deal with highly charged situations in the role of negotiator, mediator, helper and confidant. Basic psychological skills would inevitably be necessary to manage those cases to their own satisfaction. The group spoke about difficulties with clients, judges, colleagues, also about team development, migration, gender issues, ethical problems and personal problems with the feeling that trials and judgments were not always fair.

As in Balint group work with other professions, the diversity of different perspectives brought previously unknown solving strategies and relief, which in addition to increasing self-awareness helped develop and recapture passion and self-confidence to deal with problems and clients.

It is likely that we shall hear much more from lawyers and other professionals in terms of their experience with Balint group work.

Chapter 14

Summary

Balint's idea and intention to implant the psychological dimension more and more consciously into the working processes of medicine still has positive resonance today. Balint group work with medical specialists is well known, appreciated and practiced all over the world. And increasingly people from other helping social professions are interested in using this method to analyze and to improve their professional relationships.

It is apparent that this profound interest is an answer to an unbalanced reductionist scientific and functional view in our technical age.

Balint was a natural scientist and psychoanalyst and was able to synthesize seemingly polar opposites into a mutually complementing and more holistic concept.

People who work in the above mentioned professions have the advantage of presenting their problems with professional relationships to the groups and profit by it, as qualitative research in this field, mainly with self-assessment questionnaires, shows.

The investigations also show that the role of the Balint group leader is important, and that the quality of the leaders' training and supervision is inevitably fundamental.

Systemic thinking has influenced our psychotherapeutic methods of diagnoses and treatment today. From the Freudian concept of intra-psychic conflict to Balint's interpersonal model and now to the complex systemic view, our work in Balint groups has taken up this challenge and integrated methods from modern psychotherapy into the group work.

The Balint method of analytical consideration brings us back to the complexity and pleasure of interacting in the professional context.

Bibliography

Balint M (1930) Crises of the Medical Practice (2002) *American Journal of Psychoanalysis*, 1: 7–15

Balint M (1957/1972) *The Doctor, His Patient and the Illness*. International Universities Press, Inc., New York [Quoted matter throughout refers to the 1972 reprinted edition]

Balint M (1965/2001) *Primary Love and Psycho-Analytic Technique*. Routledge, Hove

Balint M (1968/1979) *The Basic Fault: Therapeutic Aspects of Regression*. Routledge, Hove

Balint Journal (2000–2016) Years 1–17. Georg Thieme Verlag, Stuttgart and New York

Bauer J (2004) Die Freiburger Schulstudie Juli 2004, www.psychotherapie-prof-bauer.de [homepage] (24 March 2011)

Engel GL (1977) The Need for a New Medical Model: A Challenge for Biomedicine. *Science*, 196 (8 April): 129–136

Ferenczi S (1932) Ohne Sympathie keine Heilung (Das klinische Tagebuch von 1932) Deutsche Erstausgabe: S. Fischer, Frankfurt am Main 1988, ISBN 3-10-020502-2, Taschenbuchausgabe: Fischer-Taschenbuch-Verl, Frankfurt am Main 1999, ISBN 3-596-14269-5, Fischer Frankfurt am Main 1999, ISBN 3-596-14269-5

Flatten G, Möller H, Tschuschke V (2015) Designing the Doctor–Patient Relationship – How Beneficial Are Balint Groups and for Whom? Proceedings of the 1st International Balint Conference, Yerevan

Freud S (1935) *A General Introduction to Psycho-Analysis*. Liveright, New York [first published in German (1917)]

Freud S (1938) *The Psychopathology of Everyday Life*. Penguin, London [first published in German (1901)]

Freud S (1938) *Totem and Taboo*. Penguin, London [first published in German (1913)]

Freud S (1976) *The Interpretation of Dreams*. Penguin, Harmondsworth [first published in German (1900)]

Freud S (1976) *Jokes and Their Relation to the Unconscious*. Penguin, Harmondsworth [first published in German (1905)]
Freud S (1977) *Three Essays on the Theory of Sexuality*. Penguin, Harmondsworth [first published in German (1905)]
Fritzsche K, Scheib P, Wirsching M, Schüler G, Wu W, Cat NH, Vongphrachanh S, Linh NT and the ASIA-LINK Workgroup (2008) Improving the Psychosomatic Competence of Medical Doctors in China, Vietnam and Laos – the ASIA-LINK Program. *International Journal of Psychiatry in Medicine*, 38: 1–11
Häfner S (2007) *Die Balintgruppe*. Deutscher Ärzteverlag, Cologne
Häfner S, Otten H, Petzold ER (2009) Some Remarks on Theory and Practice of Balint Group Work. Proceedings of the 16th International Balint Congress, Brasov
Herzog P (2016) Leitung von Balint-Gruppen: Ausbildung "The American Way". *Balint Journal*, 17: 87–92
Kjeldmand D (2006) *The Doctor, the Task and the Group*. Acta Universitatis Upsaliensis, Uppsala
Krüger RT (1997) *Kreative Interaktion*. Vandenhoeck & Ruprecht, Göttingen
Luban-Plozza B, Otten H, Petzold U, Petzold ER (1998) *Grundlagen der Balintarbeit*. Adolf Bonz Verlag, Leinfelden-Echterdingen
Maoz B, Rabin S, Matalon A (2007) The Conflict between Balint Research and the Balint Experience in Israel. Proceedings of the 15th International Balint Congress, Lisbon
Mattke D, Schäder S, Akyürek P, Spindler C (2009) Über den gezielten Einsatz der "Droge Anwalt". *Balint-Journal*, 4: 83–86
Moreau-Ricaud M (2000) *Michael Balint, Le renouveau de l'école de Budapest*. Edition érès, Toulouse
Moreno JL (1974) *Psychodrama und Soziometrie*. Essentielle Schriften, 2. Auflage (2001) Edition Humanistische Psychologie, Bergisch Glattbach
Nease D (2005) Researching the "Pharmacology" of Balint Work in the United States. Proceedings of the 14th International Balint Congress, Stockholm
Nease D, Margo K, Floyd M (2009) The Resident Balint Outcomes Study – Final Results of Our 2 Year Evaluation. Proceedings of the 16th International Balint Congress, Brasov
Obliers R, Köhle K, Kaerger H, Faber J, Koerfer A, Mendler TM, Waldschmidt T (1996) Video-Dokumentation als Instrument der Qualitätssicherung: Evaluation der Entwicklung ärztlichen Gesprächsverhaltens nach Balint-Gruppenteilnahme. In: Bahrs O, Fischer-Rosenthal W, Szecsenyi J (eds) *Vom Ablichten zum Im-Bilde-Sein. Ärztliche Qualitätszirkel und Video-Analysen*. Königshausen & Neumann, Würzburg, pp. 261–290
Otten H (2012) *Professionelle Beziehungen*. Springer, Berlin Heidelberg
Otten H, Petzold ER (2015) *The Student, the Patient and the Illness*. Foundation Psychosomatic and Social Medicine, Liestal, Switzerland

Petzold ER, Otten H (2010) *The Student, the Patient and the Illness.* Xlibri, Bloomington

Rappe-Giesecke K (2000) Vorwärts zu den Wurzeln – Balintgruppenarbeit aus kommunikationswissenschaftlicher Sicht. *Balint Journal*, 1: 36–42

Rosin U (1989) Balint-Gruppen: Konzeption, Forschung, Ergebnisse. In: *Die Balintgruppe in Klinik und Praxis.* Vol. 3. Springer, Heidelberg Berlin

Salinsky J (2001) Michael Balint Memorial Lecture: Balint Groups and Psychoanalysis: What Have the Romans Done for Us? Lecture for the Royal College of General Practitioners, London [Balintgruppen und Psychoanalyse; "Was haben die Römer für uns getan?". In: PdP 3/2010, Schattauer-Verlag, ISSN 1618-7830]

Salinsky J, Sackin P, Pinder R (2005) Studying the Balint Group: An Ethnographic Approach. Proceedings of the 14th International Balint Congress, Stockholm

Schüffel W (1988) *Sprechen mit Kranken. Erfahrungen studentischer Anamnesegruppen.* Urban & Fischer, Munich

Shoenberg P, Yakeley J (2014) *Learning about Emotions in Illness: Integrating Psychotherapeutic Teaching into Medical Education.* Routledge, Oxford

Stoffel J (2003) An jedem Zahn häng ein ganzer Mensch. *Balint Journal*, 4: 56–60

Stubbe M, Petzold ER (1996) *Beziehungserlebnisse im Medizinstudium.* Schattauer-Verlag, Stuttgart

Stucke W (1991) *Die Leitung von Balint-Gruppen.* Deutscher Ärzte Verlag, Cologne

Trenkel A (1998) Das ärztliche Gespräch bei Balint – Versuch einer Wesensbestimmung des therapeutischen Dialogs. In: Luban-Plozza B et al. (eds) *Grundlagen der Balintarbeit.* Adolf Bonz-Verlag, Leinfelden-Echterdingen

Trenkel A (2000) Zur Beziehung von Praxis und Theorie in der Balint-Arbeit. *Balint Journal*, 1: 3–7

Vinokur V (2003) Evaluation of the Effectiveness of Balint Groups in Different Social Professionals. Proceedings of the 13th International Balint Congress, Berlin

Von Weizsäcker V (1987) *Der Arzt und der Kranke, Gesammelte Schriften Bd 5.* Suhrkamp, Frankfurt am Main

Index